MILLER'S
POTTERY
Antiques Checklist

Consultant: Gordon Lang

General Editors:
Judith and Martin Miller

MILLER'S

MILLER'S ANTIQUES CHECKLIST: POTTERY

Consultant: Gordon Lang

First published in Great Britain in 1995 by Miller's,
a division of Mitchell Beazley,
both imprints of Octopus Publishing Group Ltd.
2–4 Heron Quays
Docklands
London E14 4JP

Miller's is a registered trademark of Octopus Publishing Group Ltd.

Series Editor	Alison Starling
Editor	Katie Piper
Executive Art Editor	Larraine Shamwana
Designer	David Worden
Illustrator	Amanda Patton
Special Photography	Ian Booth
Indexer	Hilary Bird
Production	Heather O'Connell
American Consultant	Nicholas M. Dawes

A CIP catalogue record for this book is available
from the British Library

ISBN 1 84000 293 X

Set in Caslon 540, Caslon 224 bold and Caslon 3
Produced by Toppan Printing Co., (HK) Ltd.
Printed and bound in China

Jacket: *A Ralph Wood pastoral group, c.1770-80, Burslem in Staffordshire*
Half-title page: *A large Adam and Eve delftware charger, c.1660, London*

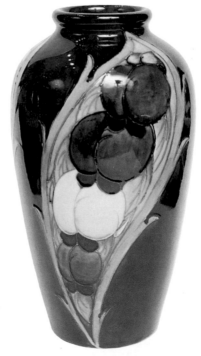

A Moorcroft Wisteria Peacock Feather design vase, c.1928

CONTENTS

BRITISH & IRISH POTTERY

AMERICAN POTTERY

FAKES & MARKS

GLOSSARY 178

BIBLIOGRAPHY 182

INDEX 183

PICTURE CREDITS & ACKNOWLEDGMENTS 190

HOW TO USE THIS BOOK

When I first started collecting antiques although there were many informative books on the subject I still felt hesitant when it came to actually buying an antique. What I really wanted to do was to interrogate the piece – to find out what it was and whether it was genuine.

The *Pottery* Checklist will show you how to assess a piece as an expert would, and provides checklists of questions you should ask before making a purchase. The answer to most (if not all) of the questions should be "yes", but remember there are always exceptions to the rule: if in doubt, seek expert guidance.

The book is divided into collecting categories, examining pottery from China and the Far East, the Islamic world, Italy, France, Germany, Holland, Britain, the United States and many other areas. At the back of the book are a bibliography, a comprehensive glossary, a list of principal makers and marks, and a section on fakes and copies for each collecting area.

Treat the book as a knowledgeable companion, and soon you will find that antique collecting is a matter of experience, and of knowing how to ask the right questions.

JUDITH MILLER

Each double-page spread looks at items belonging to a particular category of collecting.

The first page shows a carefully-chosen representative item of a type that can usually be found at antiques stores or auction houses (rather than only in museums).

The caption gives the date and dimensions of the piece shown, and a code for the price range of this type of article.

A checklist of questions gives you the key to recognizing, dating and authenticating antique pieces of the type shown.

URBINO & RELATED WARE

An Urbino istoriato dish depicting the Rape of Pr(...) dia. 12in (30.5cm); value code A

Identification checklist for Urbino and r(...)
1. Is the piece relatively thinly potted?
2. Is the glaze a warm, off-white tone?
3. Are there irregular areas of bluish or(...) in the glaze on the underside?
4. Is the decoration narrative?
5. Is the painting finely executed, but n(...) mechanical?
6. Do the colours include copper green, olive brown, black (actually an extremel(...) and a bright cobalt blue?
7. Is the rim painted in yellow ochre?

Istoriato wares
Urbino and the nearby towns of Castel Durante and Gubbio were the home of *istoriato* maiolica, where the entire surface of a piece was painted with a religious or mythological subject. From about 1520 onwards, the potters in this region made considerable quantities of narrative wares, often based on a collection of stories by the Roman

writer, Ovid (4(...)
the Metamor(...)
was extremely(...)
and painters a(...)
Renaissance.
nents of *istoria(...)*
da Urbino, his(...)
Durantino, an(...)
Francesco Xar(...)
The dish in(...)
a good exampl(...)

76

Useful background
information is
provided about the
craftsman, factory or
type of ware.

The second page
shows you what
details to look for.

tradition. By the 16thC the
decoration had become more
important than the shape of the
piece, and the dish has simply
been used as a canvas. This piece
was painted by Nicola Gabriele
Sbraghe, who often signed his
work "Nicola da Urbino," who
was perhaps the greatest exponent of *istoriato*.
* By this time, the palette of
brown, green, ochre and blue has
been joined by a rich, amber-yellow, giving a brighter feel than
Faentine *istoriato* wares.
* Also note the human forms,
which are more animated, and the
greater fluidity of the painting as
a whole.

16thC. The maiolica made there
in the first 30 years of the 16thC,
probably under the patronage of
the Dukes of Urbino, is some of
the most beautiful and influential
pottery ever made.
   The flat dish or *tagliere*, below
left, dated 1539 forms part of a
confinement set that was used to
serve food to women during the
final stages of pregnancy. It is
appropriately painted with a
mother holding her infant.
* The rim is decorated with
trophies on a blue ground, a
popular theme on Castel
Durante and Urbino wares
from about 1550 onwards.

Hints and tips help
you to assess factors
that affect value –
for example,
condition and
availability.

Gubbio
Gubbio maiolica was renowned
for its gold and ruby-lustre decoration, especially c.1600-30,
where the technique was practised successfully by Maestro
Giorgio Andreoli.

Another Urbino piece, this
dish (above) c.1530, features
Europa and the Bull, a favourite
theme for *istoriato* painters,
although they usually appear
accompanied by other figures.
* The rim is heightened in
yellow ochre, a common colour
on *istoriato* from Urbino and
other pottery towns along the
north-eastern coast of Italy, such
as Venice, Pesaro and Rimini.

Castel Durante
South west of Urbino, Castel
Durante was the home of many
great *istoriato* painters during the

Giorgio Andreoli and his
sons highlighted conventional
polychrome wares, either from
their own workshop or sent from
Urbino, in red and gold lustre.
This example, dated 1524, bears
the arms of Vigeri of Savona
within a wide border. The only
colours used underneath the
lustre were cobalt blue and
green, the remainder is either
gold or ruby lustre.
   It is usual for Andreoli to
inscribe the reverse with his
monogram and the date as he
has done on this dish.

Further photographs
show:
* items in a similar
style made in the
same area or by
the same factory
* similar, but perhaps
less valuable wares
that may be mistaken
for the more
collectable type
* common variations
on the piece shown
in the main picture
* similar wares by
other craftsmen
* the range of shapes
or decorative motifs
associated with a
particular factory,
region or period.

Later 16thC decoration
In the latter half of the 16thC
the grotesque (see glossary)
played an increasing role in decoration. First confined to borders,
as seen in the lustreware dish
above, it was eventually incorporated into the main or central
theme, reducing it in importance.

77

Marks, signatures
and serial numbers
are explained.

The codes are as follows:

A £25,000+ ($37,500+)
B £15-25,000 ($22,500-37,500)
C £10-15,000 ($15-22,500)
D £5-10,000 ($7,500-15,000)

E £2-5,000 ($3-7,500)
F £1-2,000 ($1,500-3,000)
G £500-1,000 ($750-1,500)
H under £500 (under $750)

INTRODUCTION

The making of pottery, together with basketry, is one of man's oldest accomplishments, and it is arguable which of these two crafts came first. Apart from a few fragmentary remains which have been miraculously preserved, basket-work does not by its nature survive the inevitable decay of organic or vegetable matter. Pottery too, is subject to deterioration, but here the process infinitely slower, requiring the elemental agencies of erosion or weathering to break it down. Pottery is therefore a symbol of man's ability to fashion the world for his or her own ends, indeed, it is one of the measures of a settled society. This, together with the domestication of livestock, the production of crops, and the use of polished flint tools, are the yardsticks of the earliest civilizations. It was during the Neolithic period that some communities decided to abandon the nomadic life and settle in an area where they could exercise some control over their environment, and it is duing this period that the first pottery is found.

Fired pottery, as one eminent archaeologist observed, "is very easy to break, but very difficult to destroy". It is this indestructible nature that enables pottery to furnish us with evidence of our forebears, giving us insights into what they ate and drank, the rituals that they observed, and the fashions and preoccupations of the day. For example, tomb pottery from the Han dynasty of China (209 BC-220 AD) tells us that at this time the Chinese people were influenced by three major themes. In the first period, the presence of figures of soldiers in the tombs indicates their concern with maintaining a strong military readiness for dealing with invaders. An emphasis on courtly recreation and entertain-ment characterizes the second period, and is evidence of a quieter era. In the final phase of the Han dynasty, pottery models reflect the domestic life of the ordinary person, and include animals, pig pens, well heads, barns and other farm buildings, which give us a vivid picture of everyday, rural life. Italian maiolica is another example, and the great collections on display in London and New York provide a colourful impression of the tastes of 16thC Italian society. The decoration found on pottery from this period clearly shows a fascination for Classical Roman designs and literature. Turning to the 17thC, we witness the coming-together of China and the West. It is obvious that people in northern Europe greatly admired Oriental pottery, and most pieces of Dutch, French, German or English pottery made at this time show a clear Chinese influence.

Pottery therefore speaks to us of a social context, and while we may admire the beauty of an object, or the great skill of the potter in its manufacture, knowledge of this background can only enhance our appreciation of the sub-jects as a whole. This additional interest accounts for the fact that collectors often pay very large sums for any piece that can be linked to an historical figure, such as Napoleon,

Nelson or George Washington. For those with less to spend, it is possible to put together a most interesting group of pottery wares for a relatively small outlay. The pottery market is subject to trends as well as the prevailing economic climate, and prices do fluctuate. Over the past decade the marketplace has changed considerably, but prices have become more settled. With a certain amount of knowledge, the right pieces can be obtained for reasonable sums. When beginning a collection of pottery it is important to gain real, first-hand experience of the way genuine examples of different types of pottery feel, and how they look close to. A good understanding of the material, glaze and techniques used in pottery making is fundamental, and a knowledge of form and decoration is also very important.

The best way to begin collecting pottery is to use a systematic approach, combining a study of the pieces in museums, with handling pottery at auction previews, and examining items for sale by dealers. Once some familiarity with pottery has been acquired, reading specialist books and publications will be very helpful. A knowledge of how certain pieces look and feel is necessary before full benefit can be gained from further reading. It is also important when studying a particular type of pottery, or group of wares, to target and learn from those pieces which are documentary, ie. signed and dated examples that are unquestionably authentic. Documentary wares form the basis of research on antique pottery.

A study of marks is an interesting way to learn about the evolution of pottery making. Early wares from Europe, the Far East or the Middle-East are rarely marked, except from occasional inscriptions by individual potters. Systematic marking by potters or factories is a relatively recent phenomenon, and was almost exclusive to Europe until the 19thC. In Europe, the first potters to inscribe their work were makers of Italian maiolica from about 1500, but signed and dated pieces are extremely rare. Dutch tin-glazed pottery or Delft ware, began to carry factory marks (although not on every piece), from the third quarter of the 17thC. Usually the mark comprises the initials of the proprietor, or a stylized drawing or device. Many factories in Europe producing tin-glazed wares used initials, sometimes a single letter. This can be very misleading, and a good handbook of marks is an essential companion. Great care must be taken because some reproductions have been made using early marks – there are some very deceptive pieces of French faience and Dutch Delft.

This book examines a very wide range of pottery from almost every important pottery-producing centre. In most cases, the items illustrated regularly appear at auction or are available to buy in antiques shops, but a number of exceptional pieces have been used, where they provide a good example of a particular style or type of decoration.

GORDON LANG

BASICS

Pottery is distinguished from porcelain by its coarser texture. There are two main types of pottery, porous earthenware, and non-porous stoneware. Pottery is further classified by the type of glaze, the surface of the body, and the method of decoration used.

BODY
The type of pottery body produced depends on the temperature at which an item is fired in the kiln.

* *Earthenware* is fired in the "low temperature" range, under 2200°F (1200°C). Most clays are suitable for earthenwares, and the colour of the fired body may be white, buff, brown, red or grey, depending on the natural colour of the clay and also its iron content.

* *Stoneware* is fired at 2500°F (1400°C), and the clays used must be capable of retaining their form at this temperature. During firing, the part of the clay comprised by rock melts, forming a barrier to liquids. The material is strong, hard-wearing, water-tight and can be slightly translucent. First developed in China before the 1stC AD, stoneware was also developed independently in Germany during the Middle Ages.

GLAZES
Pottery glazes are used to make a piece waterproof, in the case of earthenware, or may just be decorative. They can be translucent, opaque or coloured.
There are three principal glazes.

* *Lead glaze*: a transparent, glassy, tight-fitting glaze used on most European earthenwares, such as Staffordshire "tortoiseshell" wares, and Bernard Palissy's naturalistic flatwares, as well as Chinese Tang wares. Lead glaze may also be coloured by the addition of metal oxides.

Another well-known lead-glazed ware is cream-coloured earthenware, developed by Josiah Wedgwood in England in the 18thC. It is a very hard-bodied, cream-coloured material covered in a thin, lead glaze. Thinly potted and durable, this "creamware" supplanted tin-glazed earthenware made all over Europe (see below). In France it was termed *faience fine*. Associated with this type of pottery is "pearlware", a more refined creamware with a distinctive bluish cast, probably developed by Wedgwood in the 1770s. Another type from the same family is Prattware, a creamware decorated with high-fired colours including ochre, green, brown and blue, which sometimes has black detailing. Prattware was produced in Staffordshire, Yorkshire and Scotland, mainly at the beginning of the 19thC.

* *Tin glaze*: contains tin oxide, which gives the glaze an opaque white finish. Tin was used as an ingredient in glazing in the Middle East before the 1stC AD but it was not until about the 8th or 9thC that it appears in the guise later known throughout Europe as maiolica (Italy), faience (France and Germany), Delft ware (Holland) and delftware (England). With few exceptions, the body of most low-fired pottery varies from a strong red-brick colour through pinkish-buff to a pale greyish or off-white colour. The arrival of the earliest porcellaneous white wares from China probably in the 8th or early 9thC almost certainly encouraged potters to reproduce the effect, if not the material, by covering their local clays with a white glaze.

Opaque tin-glaze truly developed in Mesopotamia and from there the technique was carried abroad by migrating potters to North Africa, Spain, Italy, and, ultimately, to the rest of Europe.

Maiolica, faience or delftware are all made from the same ingredients; a relatively low-fired, secondary clay, which is then covered in glaze composed of oxides of lead, with a very small percentage of tin. In the firing process, the vessel, dish or tile is fired to its normal warm-coloured biscuit state, then it is removed from the kiln and glazed. Once the glaze has been absorbed into the grainy surface it is ready for decoration. After it has been coloured, the vessel or dish may be left as it is, in a matt state, or given a final dressing in a clear lead-glaze which gives the surface a brilliant, lustrous appearance.

* *Salt glaze*: formed by throwing salt into the kiln at about 2300-2500°F (1300-1400°C) during the firing of stoneware. The sodium in the salt combined with silicates in the body to form a thick glassy glaze. The addition of red lead made the glaze thicker and more glass-like. In Germany, early salt-glazed wares were made in grey and brown. In England and the United States, brown and white salt-glazed wares were produced, the latter resembling porcelain. English salt-glaze from the mid-18thC is light buff in colour with a dimpled "orange skin" surface.

SURFACE

The surface of pottery often features distinctive characteristics.
* *Crackling*: the surface of lead-glazed wares often features a network pattern, owing to the fact that the glaze does not form a natural bond with the body, and also cools at a different rate.
* *Iridescence*: the structure of lead glaze is prone to break down over time into layers, which give an iridescent or "rainbow" effect. This is particularly evident on very old pottery like Chinese Han or Tang dynasty pieces.
* *"Pinholes"*: minute air bubbles sometimes produce small holes in the glaze; this effect can also be caused by variations in the thickness of the glaze.

DECORATION
Underglaze blue
This technique was first used on Chinese porcelain, where cobalt oxide was used to decorate the piece before it was glazed. On firing, the black oxide turned blue, the shade depending on the composition of the ore. In Europe, underglaze blue was first used to decorate Delft and delft-wares with Chinoiserie designs, and use continued into the 19thC.

Underglaze colours
Known as "high temperature" or *grand-feu* colours, this range is so-called because of its ability to withstand a temperature of 2200-2400°F (1200-1300°C). The colours are from antimony (yellow), iron (brown), manganese (purple) and copper (green).

Overglaze enamels
Fired at a lower temperature than *grand-feu* colours (1300-1750°F,

700-950°C), this method, known as *petit-feu*, gives a much greater range. Enamel colours were made by adding metallic oxides to molten glass, and reducing the cooled mixture to a fine powder. This was then mixed with an oily base, painted onto the surface, and then fused by firing.

Slip decoration
*Sgraffiato: a sharp, pointed tool is used to cut through a layer of slip (liquid clay with a creamy consistency, applied using a nozzle), to the pottery body underneath. Used throughout Europe on earthenware on stoneware, this technique was also used in the United States.
* *Slip combing*: two colours of slip are combed over one another to give a feathered effect.
* *Slip trailing*: the body is trailed with slip in a colour contrasting to the ground colour of the piece.

Other techniques
* *Sprigging*: relief decoration moulded from slip is added to the surface of a piece before firing.
* *Stamping*: a pad of contrasting clay is applied to the body and a design stamped onto it. The excess clay is removed when dry.
* *Piercing*: the unfired body is marked with a design that is then cut out using a knife.
* *Metallic lustre*: shiny, metallic decoration with the appearance of copper or silver.
* *Sponging*: the piece is daubed with a sponge giving a mottled effect after firing. Popular in the United States 1825-50, pottery with this type of decoration was known as "spatterware".

Decorative influences
* *Chinoiserie*: Chinese-style decoration or motifs were a major influence on Western pottery, and include temples, lakes, fishermen and bridges.
* *Famille rose*: a colour range or palette of enamels developed on Chinese porcelain, which includes a distinctive rose-pink. Used in Europe in the 18thC.
* *Famille verte*: an enamel palette dominated by green. Its popularity was eclipsed by *famille rose*.
* *Imari*: a type of Japanese porcelain made from the beginning of the 17thC based on native textiles, with a palette dominated by a strong blue and red. Copied in Europe in the 18th and 19thC.

POTTERY COLOURS

The colours used to decorate pottery often provide an important clue to the date or origin of a particular piece. In Italy, for example, the variation between the colours found on the relatively small number of marked items from the different pottery-producing regions throughout the country, can help to classify unmarked wares.

turquoise (Iznik, Turkey mid-16th-end 17thC)

green-blue (Urbino *istoriato*, Italy c.1525-75)

deep blue (Faenza, Italy c.1525-50)

red "sealing wax red" (Iznik, Turkey mid-16th-end 17thC)

mid-range cobalt (Venice and Urbino *istoriato*, Italy 16thC)

greyish-cobalt (Deruta, Italy c.1520-50)

lustre (Spain 15th-16thC)

yellow (Italy 17thC)

sienna (Deruta, Siena, Italy early 16thC)

manganese brown (Italy, Spain 15th-16thC)

ruby lustre (Gubbio, Italy c.1500-55)

yellow-green (Urbino, Italy c.1520-50)

It would be impossible to chart all the colours and tones used in all areas during all periods of production, especially since more than two colours were often painted over one another creating a completely different shade. These two pages include some of the most characteristic pottery colours, together with the area and the period in which they were used. Please note that the colours shown below are designed to act as a guide only.

ochre (Deruta, Italy c.1500-25)

dark blue (Nevers, France 1650-1700)

turquoise (Italy late 15thC, English delftware 17thC)

grey-green (Castelli, Siena, Italy 18thC)

red (France, Holland, London 18thC)

yellow (English delftware late 17th and 18thC)

stone (Urbino, Italy c.1525-75)

ochre (Holland early 17thC)

grey-blue (English delftware late 17th and 18thC)

puce "purple manganese" (Strasbourg, France c.1750-1800)

grey-green (English delftware 18thC)

mid-blue (English delftware late 17th and 18thC)

POTTERY FORMS

Many of the forms made by the main pottery-producing centres are
very distinctive, and a familiarity with these types of wares and the
areas in which they were produced, can be of help to a collector

Helmet-shaped ewer,
Rouen, France 18thC

Two-handled jar,
Florence, Italy 15thC

Covered jug, Orsini-
Colonna, Italy 16thC

Two-handled vase,
Deruta, Italy 16thC

Wet drug-jar, Castel
Durante, Italy 16thC

Pharmacy bottle,
Italy 16thC

Pilgrim flask, Urbino,
Italy 16thC

Oviform jar, Venice,
Italy 16thC

Oviform albarello,
Palermo, Sicily 17thC

Campana-shaped
vase, Italy, 18thC

Pharmacy jar, Savona,
Italy 17thC

Tankard, Annaberg,
Germany 17thC

when attributing a particular piece. Illustrated here are a number of identifiable forms, together with their country of origin and a guide to the period in which they were made. Please note that these items are not drawn to scale, and comparisons between the size of the objects should not be made.

Apostelhumpen, Kreussen, Germany 17thC

Stoneware jug, Germany late 16thC

Bartmannkrug, Frechen, Germany 16thC

Stoneware jug, Raeren, Germany 16thC

Jug, Westerwald, Germany 17thC

Schnelle, Siegburg, Germany 16thC

Enghalskrug, Hanau, Germany 18thC

Tureen, Strasbourg, France 18thC

Jug, Delft, Holland 18thC

Vase, Delft, Holland 18thC

Posset pot, Bristol, England 18thC

Agateware vase, England, 18thC

CHINESE POTTERY

A Han dynasty, green-glazed watchtower, c.150AD

Chinese Neolithic cultures were located around the Shandong Peninsula, along the Gansu Corridor, and as far as the Gobi Desert and beyond (see map on pp.18-19). There were two early cultures that produced notable pottery wares. First, the Gansu Yangshao culture (3000-1500 BC) made large, hand-made, refined funerary wares in red clay, decorated with red, black and brown pigments. Second, the Longshan culture (3000-1700 BC) in Shandong appear to be the first Neolithic people to use the fast-turning wheel (c.2000 BC). They made blackware vessels with angular profiles, which, once again, were mainly funerary items.

The first historical period of China was the Shang dynasty (1700-1027 BC). During this period, potters benefited from bronze technology and developed high-firing kilns which led to the production of the first white-clayed wares. It was about this time that the first, accidental, glazes appeared, caused by burnt wood ash rising with the hot air of the kiln, and settling on the upper halves of vessels. Also at around this time, potters began to look at other decorative media for inspiration, especially items made from bronze.

During the Han dynasty (206 BC-220 AD) there were two important advances. First was the development of high-fired stonewares, also known as proto-porcelain. Second was the use of lead glaze, which produced a very distinctive, dark, emerald green, although most glazed pieces that exist today feature some surface iridescence due to burial over a long period. At this time, pottery figures even replaced the need for human sacrifice in the burial ceremony. Possibly the last example of human sacrifice, is the Terracotta Army of the first Qin emperor (Qin Shihuang 259-210 BC). Also found in tombs during this period were pottery replicas of everyday objects – bronze wares, and other symbolic items, such as the watchtower shown opposite. Watchtowers were a very important feature of everyday life, offering protection to villagers who were vulnerable to attack by nomads who succeeded in scaling the Great Wall. In addition, pottery models of wells, gateways, cattle pens, and domestic and wild animals are found.

Around 300 AD the first, high-fired, green stonewares began to appear. These were to develop into the celebrated Yue wares (see pp.24-5), and subsequently into celadon (see pp.26-9). During the Tang dynasty (618-906 AD) there were two distinct types of pottery: greenwares, and low-fired, refined vessels made from white clay, a material that had fallen out of use since the end of the Shang dynasty (see above). It was these white wares which were the basis of the development of porcelain in China. Many pottery figures were made during the Tang dynasty, and these are extremely popular with collectors of Chinese ceramics (see pp.22-3). The variety of coloured glazes increased at this time, and the potter was able to work in ochre, white and blue, as well as green, brown and black. This colour range is known as *sancai*.

The Song dynasty (960-1279) marks a watershed in Chinese pottery. The period is regarded as the classic period of production, with its subtle forms, often based on flowers, and beautiful green, white and black glazes. The celadons produced at this time were of such high quality that they outclassed the wares made by the emerging porcelain manufacturers.

From the Yuan dynasty (1279-1368) onwards, with the refinement of porcelain production and its growing popularity, pottery production declined, and pottery itself became regarded merely as a utilitarian material. Some lead-glazed wares however, such as roof tiles, have retained an architectural importance, and are still produced today.

CHINESE CENTRES

LIANOING

Beijing ▲

HEBEI

SHANDONG

nyang

JIANGSU

ANHUI

ZHEJIANG

JIANGXI

FUJIAN

DONG
angzhou

Chinese periods and dynasties
As well as classification by type of
ware, Chinese pottery is often
categorized according to the
period or dynasty in which it was
produced. Listed below are the
names of the main periods of
Chinese history together with
their corresponding dates.

Neolithic cultures

Peiligang	c.6500-5000 BC
Cishan	c.6500-5500 BC
Central Yangshao	c.5000-3000 BC
Gansu Yangshao	c.3000-1500 BC
Dawenkou	c.5800-1500 BC
Hogshan	c.4000-2700 BC
Majiabang	c.5500-3000 BC
Songze	c.3500-2500 BC
Hemudu	c.5200-3000 BC
Daxi	c.5500-3500 BC
Longshan	c.3000-1700 BC

Early dynasties

Shang	c.1700-1027 BC
Western Zhou	1027-771 BC
Eastern Zhou	
Spring and Autumn	
period	771-481 BC
Warring States	
period	480-221 BC

Imperial China

Qin	221-207 BC
Han	
Western Han	206 BC-9 AD
Xin	9-25 AD
Eastern Han	25-220 AD
Three Kingdoms	
Shu (Han)	221-263
Wei	220-265
Wu	222-280
Southern dynasties	
(Six Dynasties)	
Western Jin	265-316
Eastern Jin	317-420
Liu Song	420-479
Southern Qi	479-502
Liang	502-557
Chen	557-589
Northern dynasties	
Northern Wei	386-535
Eastern Wei	534-550
Western Wei	535-557
Northern Qi	550-577
Northern Zhou	557-581
Sui	581-618
Tang	618-906
Liao	907-960
Song	
Northern Song	960-1126
Southern Song	1127-1279
Jin	1115-1234
Yuan	1279-1368
Ming	1368-1644
Qing	1644-1916

EARLY CHINESE POTTERY

*A Neolithic funerary jar, c.3000 BC;
ht 12⅖in (31cm); value code E.*

Identification checklist for Neolithic Yangshao Chinese pottery (c.3000 BC)
1. Has the piece been hand-coiled?
2. Is the body very thin?
3. Does the piece have wide shoulders?
4. Is the piece painted in black or purple?
5. Does the decoration include bold striped, geometric or animal motifs?
6. Has the lower half of the piece been left undecorated?
7. If there are handles, are they attached just below the mid-point along the sides of the piece?

Neolithic pottery
Pottery from the Neolithic cultures of northern and southern China is among the earliest efforts of man to shape clay into useful and decorative forms. Although the first specimens so far discovered can be dated to about 7,000 BC, few examples of this period are known outside China. Collectors in the West are more familiar with pieces from the later Neolithic cultures of the Shandong peninsula dating from about 4300-2400 BC and of the Yangshao of central and northern China, which dates from about 5000-1500 BC.

* These distinctive types do appear on the market, and are surprisingly inexpensive considering their great age.

Funerary wares
Although a variety of vessels were made for cooking, drinking or storage, the Yangshao culture is noted for its generous, wide-shouldered funerary vessels painted in bold striped, geometric or animal motifs in black and purple pigment, such as the piece in the main picture. These, often large, jars are hand coiled and pared down to great thinness.

* Because they were embedded in sand inside the tombs, the lower halves of these vessels were left undecorated.

Technical developments
* In the middle period of the Shandong culture some vessels were produced that show signs of wheel turning, marking the earliest use of the pottery wheel.
* During the first historical period in China, the Shang dynasty (c.1650-1027 BC) there were two further developments: the use of a fine white clay (a forerunner of porcelain), and the first evidence of glazing.

The first glaze was formed from wood ash which rose up during firing, forming a glaze where it landed. This is usually evident on the shoulders of early wares.

Period of the Warring States (481-221 BC)
The Period of the Warring States preceded the unification of China under the first Qin emperor.

Unglazed wares continued to be made during this period, such as this jar, moulded in shallow relief with squared scrolls in the manner of bronze.
* Many early Chinese wares are similar, in both shape and decoration, to contemporary bronzes. These were often used in burials, as substitutes for bronze, and also lacquer wares.

The Han Dynasty (206 BC-220 AD)
By the Han dynasty a very wide range of objects were produced, not only for funerary purposes, even if much of what has been discovered and appears on the market today has been unearthed from burial sites. Pottery was used to make replicas of objects the dead would need to take with them to the afterlife.

Potters of this period introduced the smooth green or ochre coloured lead glaze, as well as the high-fired stonewares, which eventually developed into Yue ware (see pp.24-5). The rich, green glaze is seen on this model of an oven.
* As well as ovens, Han potters also made models of buildings, gatehouses, watchtowers, barns, pig pens and animals.

Made during the later Western Han period (206-9 BC), the pyramidal form, stylized features and soft rounded contours of this kneeling figure are typical of Han modelling.
* The Western Han was largely a period of conflict and many figures made at this time had military significance. The Eastern Han (25-220 AD) was a more peaceful time, and models are more domestic.

Marks
Apart from the very rare mark of an individual potter, these early wares are unmarked.

TANG POTTERY

*One of a pair of straw-glazed figures of court ladies, Tang dynasty;
ht 12 ⅜in (31.5cm); value code E.*

Identification checklist for Tang straw-glazed figures
1. Is the figure well-modelled with soft contours and careful detailing?
2. Have facial details been highlighted with red and black pigment?
3. Does the glaze have an ivory tint?
4. Is the material pinkish-white?
5. Is the glaze crackled?
6. Is there evidence of iridescence on the surface?
7. Are there traces of earth on the body of the piece (as if the piece has been buried for a long time)?
8. Is there relatively little wear on the piece?
9. Does the glaze come right to the edge of the base of the figure?

The Tang dynasty (618-906 AD)

A considerable number of sophisticated, low-fired, white bodied wares were made during the Tang dynasty, and many have been discovered in recent years.

Figures

Figures were made in a wide variety of forms, including models of foreign visitors to China, who fascinated the potters, and figures of touring acrobats, dancers, musicians, and also Western merchants, grooms and people from many Asian tribes are found.

Male and female court figures are particularly desirable. Made in the 8thC, this model is based on Yang Guefei, the concubine of Tang Emperor Li, who was instrumental in the deaths of many of the Imperial family and the court. Her bouffant hairstyle and plump figure became fashionable, and her likeness was immortalized by Tang potters.

Figures of horses and camels were widely produced. Typically, this horse and rider is crisply-modelled and highly detailed.

Unglazed wares

Many figures were unglazed, such as the models of the concubine and the horse and rider shown above. They have the following features:
* a finely-modelled body with soft contours
* a pinkish-white, absorbent-looking body
* unglazed faces with facial details highlighted with red and black pigment.

Glazed wares

White straw-glazed and polychrome figures and wares were also made during the Tang dynasty. Straw-glazed pieces such as the court lady in the main picture, are ivory-tinted and the glaze is crackled.

Polychrome wares

Tang polychrome pieces are known as *sancai* ("three-coloured") wares, and were made in the first half of the 8thC. *Sancai*-glazes were used on figures and other wares, such as the pot below.

On vertical polychrome wares the glaze always drifts and hangs like a curtain, and the crackled lead glaze never goes neatly to the base as it does on straw-glazed wares.
* Polychrome flatwares are marked with grooves to stop the glaze from drifting during firing.
* *Sancai* figures also have unglazed faces with red and black detailing.

Collecting

The more modestly priced Tang wares are either unglazed or straw-glazed. Most glazed pieces will feature some iridescence caused by a long period of burial. As well as figures, commonly-found wares include small globular jars, cups and trays (with or without handles), footed dishes and small ewers.

YUE WARE

An early Yue funerary jar and cover, Han dynasty (206 BC-220 AD); ht 9¼in (48.7cm); value code E

Identification checklist for Yue ware
1. Is the body greyish close-grained stoneware?
2. Has the unglazed area turned reddish?
3. Is the glaze greyish-green or olive coloured?
4. Is the glaze crazed or crackled?
5. Is the glaze irregular (has it coagulated or streaked vertically)?
6. Does the glaze reach the footring (later wares do)?
7. Is there a circle of small gritty marks on the base?
8. Is the footrim shallow?

Yue Ware
Yue wares are the earliest and most influential form of Chinese stoneware. The province of Zhejiang in the east of China, has a long tradition of pottery production. The earliest green-glazed wares emanate from Yue during the 3rd or 4thC BC. This type of ware was regarded as sophisticated enough for use by the upper echelons of society, particularly the educated, and not only for the more usual domestic and funerary purposes.

Early forms include jars such as the example in the main picture, vases, basins, bowls and lamps. Some of these pieces are based on contemporary bronze forms but others, often in a highly stylized manner, are adapted from spirit or animal figures.

Technique
Because of the proportion of feldspar (a rock-forming mineral used in the production of hard paste porcelain) in Yue composition, the early wares

have been given a somewhat confusing name "Proto-porcelain", for although it is a moderately refined ware in material, glaze and potting it is still a long way from what we now consider to be "porcelain". On firing, the greyish close-grained stoneware body often develops a soft pinkish-red hue on the unglazed areas, a feature also found later on Zhejiang celadon.

More advanced than the covered jar in the main picture, this double-handled jar, probably from the 3rd or 4thC AD is a very early example of splashed ware, which probably coincides with the development of brown glazed wares in the south of China. The glaze covers most of the body but stops well above the base. The waves on the neck and shoulders between the multiple grooves are looser than on the covered jar.

This shouldered ovoid form dates from the 5thC AD (early versions are more globular). While some spouts are real, others such as this one, are merely decorative. The square cut lugs (side handles) are characteristic, as are the thinnish, waisted neck and angular, galleried mouthrim. This last feature, together with the tall animal-like handle, are found on Tang (618-906) funerary amphorae.
* The "chicken head" is seen on the left-hand side of the piece.

Later Yue wares
Yue ware continued in production until the Northern Song dynasty (960-1127), and while it was revered by scholars and connoisseurs, the sumptuously glazed celadons of Longquan, near Hangzhou became more desirable.

Decoration
Glaze is generally thin and olive-coloured and tends to assume a fine crackle. As with so many pre-Song wares the glazes terminate in an irregular wavy line well above the base. Most often the vessel is set on a shallow knife-cut footrim. Yue stoneware is supported on a ring of small clay spurs or stilts which leave clear grit-encrusted patches on the underside. Wares made in the Han period are decorated with incised free-running plant or animal designs, fine applied lines, stamped or impressed decoration, geometric repeating patterns formed using a small wheel, or with splashed, iron-brown spots.

Later pieces are identified by their bold carving, similar to that of early Song celadons and porcelains. This compact waterpot from the Five Dynasties (907-960) is typical, and is carved with peony and chrysanthemum.
* Notice how the glaze neatly fits the jar which is slightly askew, having collapsed during the firing.
* It is unusual to find any early vessel which has not sagged or warped in the firing.

Chicken Ewers
Unique to the area centred on Nanjing, "chicken-headed ewers" are found from the 4thC.

25

A Yaozhou shallow bowl, 12th-13thC;
ht 6in (15.2cm); value code E/F

Identification checklist for northern celadon
(Yaozhou ware)
1. Has the piece been made from a white or slightly off-white clay?
2. Has the footrim (where the clay is visible) oxidized to a brownish red or caramel colour?
3. Is the glaze olive green?
4. Is it thin and minutely bubbled?
5. Does the piece feature carving or moulding?
6. Is the design scrolling foliage (there are some animal and figure subjects on later pieces)?
7. If the piece is a bowl, is it supported on a neatly-cut footrim with a very small diameter?

Northern celadon

The Yaozhou kilns of Shaanxi in the north west of China were ideally placed to take advantage of their location, close to the market offered by the capital, Xian. A high proportion of Westerners lived in Xian; during this period there were as many as 100,000. These facts, together with a fine, whitish local clay and abundant supply of coal, made the production of the northern variety of celadon an economic success. This olive-green ware is easily distinguished from its southern counterpart (see pp. 28-9). Production of northern celadon began during the northern Song dynasty (960-1127), flourished until the invasion of Jurchen Tartars forced the court to flee south to Hangzhou in 1127, and production gradually declined during the Yuan period. Later Yaozhou celadon is cursory and mass-produced, being little more than "local ware".

Characteristics

Yaozhou ware is composed of fine, whitish clay and covered in a thin olive-coloured glaze. It is supported on a relatively narrow and neat footrim which will tend to oxidize a rusty caramel colour, similar to that of Junyao. Although not visible in the main picture, the bowl shown has a flattened footrim which is atypical.

Types of ware

Most of the output were open wares, dishes or bowls, a fact underlined by the large numbers of these which come on the market. Hollow wares are scarce – cup stands, ewers, vases *(meiping)*, censers, waterpots and boxes.

Decoration

This distinctive ware is especially noted for its bold sweeping carving. This style of decoration appears in the 10thC and seems to have been strongly influenced by the Yue wares of Zhejiang province (see pp.24-5), even if the predominant greyish tones of Yue are quite unlike the more olive or greenish yellow hues of Yaozhou. It is possible that the migration of potters from Yue to Shaanxi province following the fall of the ruling house in 978 was a cause of this continuity, but it is important to remember that Yue ware itself was renowned throughout China, and was used as tribute ware to the Imperial court.

Early Yaozhou wares are freely carved with relatively large scale floral subjects such as peony, chrysanthemum or lotus. There is also a strong resemblance to early Cizhou carved ware in the treatment of the cut-away and combed decoration.

As well as a decorational similarity to Cizhou wares, there are many similarities between the forms produced in the two areas. These include:
* flanged lamps
* *meiping*
* deeply-carved bowls with floral decoration
* figures of ducks and fish.

Towards the end of the 12thC moulds were introduced, as seen on this bowl from the Jin dynasty (1115-1234). A stoneware mould could be worked in greater detail than a thin piece of clay which required greater skill; designs are tight and complex, and usually comprise scrolling peony and lotus, but tend to be less spontaneous than patterns carved by hand.
* The mould for this piece was shaped like a cone.
* The advantage of moulds was that they could be used a great number of times before they wore out.
* The thin olive-green glaze dwells in the carved gulleys and sunken surfaces emphasizing the design.

The carving on this censer is crisp and deeply cut in the typical early Song style, heightening the outlines of the piece. Later, a more sophisticated but shallower treatment became popular, filling up the space and reinforcing the contours of more complicated vessels.

Probably based on an earlier, Tang dynasty (618-906 AD), silver box, this piece is carved in shallow relief with some undercutting, and a carefully placed flowerhead, a feature of many boxes. The interior has three tiny bowls probably to hold cosmetic agents.

SOUTHERN CELADON

A Longquan celadon bowl with pointed vertical ribs,
Southern Song dynasty (1127-1279); ht 3⅝in (9cm); value code E.

Identification checklist for Song and Yuan dynasty southern celadon
1. Is the paste white with a slight suggestion of grey?
2. Is there red oxidization on unglazed areas such as the footrim?
3. Is the glaze thick?
4. On close inspection (it may be useful to use a magnifying glass), does the glaze appear to be full of minute bubbles?
5. Has the footrim been trimmed with a knife (are facets visible)?
6. Is the decoration carved or moulded?
7. Is the piece thickly potted?

Southern celadon

In the declining years of Yue (see pp. 24-5), a more refined ware began to emerge from the area around Longquan, also in Zhejiang province. This area had extensive deposits of a fine white porcellaneous clay. Covered in a thick, bluish-green glaze, the name "celadon" derives from a character in a 17thC French romantic play by Honoré d'Urfe, who wore clothes that resembled this colour. The term has been adopted in the west, although in China it is called "prunus green".

The Southern Song dynasty (1127-1279)

It was not until the Southern Song dynasty that the characteristic celadon was fully developed. By then there were hundreds of kilns producing a great range of dishes and vessels for domestic and ritual purposes.

Vast quantities were also exported to South-east Asia, India, the Middle and Near East. The Sinan shipwreck, dateable to c.1323, contained over 5,000 pieces of Longquan celadon, with some pieces still neatly stacked in their containers.

There appears to be a clear division between the celadon wares exported to the Middle East, and those sold in South East Asia. While the Indian and Islamic world had a preference for large dishes, bowls and vases, there are virtually no examples of the small bowls and oil jars that have been excavated in large quantities in the Philippines and South East Asia.

Much of the revenue gained from the sale of celadon was used to fortify the northern boundaries of China against the Mongols lead by Genghis Khan during the 13thC.

Characteristics

Early wares are boldly carved much in the manner of Yue stoneware and then covered in a semi-translucent palish green glaze.

* The Longquan bowl in the main picture is a good example of one of the most common forms. Based on the half-opened lotus flower, production of this shape continued well into the Yuan period.

* The small foot is characteristic of Song ceramic bowls.

* Where the glaze is thin (on the ribs of the bowl), the white body is visible.

rendered opaque by the presence of lime and wood-ash. The glaze is so heavily applied that it softens the contours in much the same way as on Jun wares (see pp.32-33).

* Many of the forms of celadon are based on archaic bronze, jade or lacquer originals, and it is only during the Mongol Yuan dynasty (1279-1368) that bold surface decoration, either carving or moulding, began to reappear. By then the production of celadon was competing with the newly developed blue and white porcelain of Jingdezhen.

This Longquan celadon vase made during the Southern Song Dynasty, is based on one of the very oldest forms, the Cong, a Neolithic jade of about 2500 BC. The soft green glaze is designed to imitate jade, the most precious of materials to the Chinese.

* The glassy neatly-applied glaze contrasts with the more erratic efforts found on Yue wares.

* Just visible on the margin of the glaze at the foot is a band of russet oxidization found on almost every piece of Longquan celadon.

Decoration

The best celadon dates from the 12th, 13th and early 14thC; undecorated vessels and dishes supersede the earlier, more primitive, heavily carved wares. Well-potted in classical shapes, they are covered in a thick glaze,

The classic shape of this dragon dish from the Yuan dynasty. (1279-1368), first appeared in an undecorated form in the Southern Song dynasty. Changing tastes during this later period, have led to the surface of this piece being embellished with an applied dragon in low relief and vigorous wave motif, a combination which is the very antithesis of Song Longquan.

The gently wavy rim on this Longquan dish suggests that the potter was inspired by Song lacquer wares. Here the raised motifs have been left unglazed and have burnt red in the firing, a popular decorative device.

* The arrangement of three fruit is unusual.

CIZHOU STONEWARE

A Cizhou cut-glaze stoneware meiping with sgraffiato decoration, Jin/Yuan dynasty (13thC); ht 14⅛ in (36cm); value code C/D

Identification checklist for Cizhou stoneware
1. Is the body a slightly granular, buff-coloured stoneware?
2. Is the footrim clearly trimmed with a knife?
3. Is there a slip over the body (this could be either whitish or brown)?
4. Has the piece been fired on spurs, leaving small gritty patches?
5. Does the decoration comprise one or more of the following styles: incised or carved through one slip colour onto another; painted in iron-brown; painted over the glaze in red, green and possibly yellow (later wares may also have had black and brown overglaze colours); covered in a green or turquoise glaze?
6. Is the clear glaze crackled?
7. Is the piece warped?

Cizhou stoneware
Cizhou stoneware was produced mainly in the northern provinces of Henan, Hebei and Shaanxi from the early Song dynasty (960-1279) until the Ming dynasty. It is invariably decorated, in contrast to the classic Song tradition of monochrome ware, and ranges from exuberantly decorated *meiping* (a tall narrow-necked vase) to delicate, painted pillows. Cizhou ware is probably the most versatile of all medieval Chinese ceramics, and is both useful and decorative.

* In the present century Cizhou has been a source of inspiration for Bernard Leach, William Staite Murray, Michael Cardew, and many other modern studio potters.

Technique

Fired at a relatively modest 1200°C, this buff-coloured or greyish stoneware is dressed in a cream or dark brown slip under a clear slightly off-white crackled glaze.
* The object is generally crudely worked with obvious knife or tool marks, as seen in the main picture, especially on the footrim where the dark-speckled clay is faceted rather like whittled wood.
* Most pieces show some warping or twisting.

Decoration

Cizhou is decorated in a variety of ways, often combining two or more techniques. The earliest wares were finely incised and punched with floral subjects arranged in wide bands or zone. Later, painting either in brown or black on white or cream slip, was added to the range.
* Other variations on the *sgraffiato* method included cutting through one or even two slips as well as the glaze to the underlying body.

A considerable portion of Cizhou stonewares were painted in iron-brown slip on a pale ground. In keeping with the confident expansionism of the Yuan Dynasty (1279-1368), this heavy-shouldered wine jar *(guan)* is freely painted in a lively hand with dragon and phoenix designs within contoured barbed panels.
* Panels were a popular design feature during this period.
* Designs are mostly floral with bold, large-scale peonies or sweeping calligraphic vegetation.
* Rarer subjects include children playing, or later, more extensive semi-narrative subjects (almost certainly derived from contemporary graphic sources).

As demonstrated on this jar from the Song/Jin Dynasty in the 12thC, northern Chinese potters were skilled in combining decorative techniques. This piece features simple incising on the body, together with more elaborate design painted in brown slip.
* Just visible, peeping through the slip, on the edge of the foot is the slightly darker body.

Marks

In general Cizhou stonewares are unmarked, but there are some important exceptions. A group of wares made during the Jin dynasty (1115-1234), by the Zhang family from Xiang, the area surrounding the old city of Anyang in northern Henan, do bear potter's marks.

Forms

Cizhou stonewares were produced in a great variety of forms, usually conforming to standard contemporary ceramic shapes, including vases, jars, pillows, bowls, dishes boxes, cups and stands.
* Made during the Song dynasty (960-1279), this unusual Cizhou vase (8in, 20.3cm in height) has been painted with Chinese characters in black pigment.

JUN WARE

A Junyao narcissus bowl, Jin/Yuan Dynasty; dia. 12in (30.5cm); value code B/C

Identification checklist for Jun wares
1. Is the body greyish or pale buff stoneware?
2. Is the glaze thickly applied:
3. Does the glaze gather thickly above the footrim?
4. Is the glaze slightly dribbled?
5. Is there a caramel-coloured dressing covering unglazed areas?
6. Is this brownish colour visible where the glaze is thin?
7. Are there large spur marks inside the footring (this applies only to larger pieces)?
8. Is the glaze bubbled and/or crackled?
9. Is the glaze lavender coloured or splashed with purple?
10. Is the glaze flecked or brindled with a mixture of purple and lavender?
11. Are the shapes generally simple with no surface moulding or decoration (there are a few extremely rare exceptions)?
12. If there is a mark, is it a single Chinese number?

Jun stoneware
Jun stoneware was regarded during the Ming dynasty as being of Imperial status. Jun was mainly produced in Linru near Luoyang in central Henan in the north of China. However there were many other kilns in the province of Henan. These and other kilns made Jun wares of varying quality for widespread distribution. Stoutly potted, their use was not confined to the Imperial household.

* Copies of Jun ware were made in Guangdong province in southern China during the Qing dynasty.

Categories of Jun ware

Western scholars have classified Jun into four, basically chronological categories:
* green
* lavender-blue
* purple-splashed lavender-blue
* brindled glazed ware that combines purple and lavender decoration.

This vessel has a typical form with a compressed bulbous body and straight neck rolled outwards at the rim. Such pieces were probably used for ritual purposes on an altar. It is a good example of the third category of purple-splashed lavender glazed Jun.

Technique

All Jun ware is heavily potted, with a greyish stoneware body, which is then dressed in an iron wash; this is evident on rims, edges and the base when it is not glazed. Finally, the heavy glaze is applied, which tends to fall irregularly around the base of the piece in a wavy band and generous dribbles.
* On the larger vessels, a circular arrangement of numerous kiln supports or spurs can be seen inside the footrim. The blemishes or "warts" left behind when these have been snapped off reveal the greyish body.

Marks

Jun wares were sometimes numbered when a piece was made comprising two parts, using a character between one and ten.

Flower pots

A number of Jun wares were designed for growing or displaying flowers, such as the narcissus bowl in the main picture.

The narcissus bowl and this large flower pot from the Jin/Yuan dynasty represent the more complex forms of Jun ware. Some larger pieces are incised with the characters *feng hua*, the name of a pavilion in the Imperial palace at Kaifeng, the old capital of the Northern Song.
* Other Jun wares include bulb bowls, *jardinières* and tall vases *(zun)*. There are also different shapes, such as large and small bubble cups with rounded sides incurving at the lip, small tulip-shaped jars, globular jars with tiny lugs applied around the narrow mouth, plain dishes with flattened rims, and barbed dishes.
* A relatively common form during the 13th-15thC, barbed dishes were moulded with outward projecting points. This shape is also found in southern celadon.

Glaze

The glaze usually contains bubbles which give a pock-marked appearance, and it may be crackled. On some pieces the surface of the glaze features an interrupted network of lines that experts have called "worm tracks".

These bowls from the 12thC illustrate the most common Jun form. At first glance the green bowl looks deceptively like celadon, however the glaze is thicker than northern celadon and not as greasy in appearance as the southern variety. Furthermore, the base of a Jun bowl will probably be slightly pointed and the footrim relatively thick.

FAR EASTERN POTTERY

A lobed celadon ewer and cover, Koryo dynasty (918-1392)

During the 1stC AD, the power and influence of China extended as far as the Caspian sea in the west, to Vietnam and Korea in the south, and Japan to the east. By the Song dynasty (960-1279) Chinese ceramics were imitated by almost all Far Eastern countries.

Korean potters were among the first to produce accomplished stonewares, reflecting some classic wares of China. Korean celadons of the 12th and 13thC have some of the characteristics of Chinese Yue wares, and northern or Yaozhou celadon. The more popular Cizhou stonewares were also echoed in Korea at the same time, in their glaze, material and form. The wares produced in Korea included baluster vases (*meiping*), lotus bowls, cosmetic boxes, wine vessels, and cups and stands. In spite of this high degree of imitation, Korean pottery does exhibit great individuality, and can be very high quality. Unique to Korea are inlaid *mishima* wares, and coarse, slip-decorated, Punch'ong wares.

Annam (present-day Vietnam), to the south of China, produced a wide range of wares, either blue and white, polychrome or monochrome; all used the same basic, greyish porcellaneous stoneware body. Again mainly based on Chinese porcelains and stonewares, they are readily identifiable by their distinctive clay, and subtly differing forms, and brushwork and pigment if painted. Annamese wares appear to have been made largely for export as vast quantities have been excavated all over south-east Asia, particularly in Indonesia and the Philippines. The Annamese potter copied Chinese celadons, brownwares, and blue and white porcelain. Also produced were "old-fashioned" Chinese-style wares for sale in Asia; the celebrated Annamese bottle dated 1450 in the Topkapu Sarayi Museum in Istanbul in Turkey, is clearly based on a type of decoration current in the middle of the previous century in China. Items produced include small, globular oil jars, boxes and animal-shaped water droppers. Although the inspiration for the blue and white decoration is clearly Chinese, Annamese designs are idiosyncratic, and the potting is skilled but provincial. These items have a great appeal for the collector.

Thai pottery was also influenced by Chinese ceramics, particularly the celadon wares. Often elegant, with forms that include flared, lotus-shaped bowls or pear-shaped bottles, the main difference between Chinese originals and these derivative pieces, is in the body, which is made from a peppery, buff-coloured stoneware. The thickly-applied, translucent glaze is a pale, sea-green colour, which often pools towards the base, and is quite unlike the opaque, bubbled glazes of Chinese Longquan celadon. A major proportion of the production was of brown-glazed wares, similar in colour to the Chinese *temmoku* stonewares of Henan or Fujian, but with a matt, less lustrous glaze. There are two types of pottery that are peculiar to Thailand. First, there is a distinct group of *sgraffiato* wares – often covered boxes – incised with vegetal designs against a brown ground. This type is loosely akin to Chinese Cizhou ware, but only in technique. Second is a small and curious group of individually-modelled figures of humans and animals. Highly primitive, they were probably made for ritualistic purposes.

Over a long period potters in Japan drew inspiration from China. This can be seen in wares contemporary with the Tang and Song dynasties. However, the increased interest in the Tea Ceremony (see pp.40-1), encouraged generations of potters to create highly individual work, and while there are identifiable local characteristics of the different stonewares and earthenwares, attribution is hindered by isolated craftsmen working in borrowed styles. The most revered ceramics in Japan are generally associated with the "Six Old Kilns", the products of which always show the hand of the potter, unlike the more mechanized products from China. These wares have been a major influence on potters in other centres, most recently on 20thC Studio potters, such as Bernard Leach and Shoji Hamada (see pp.148-9).

The wares of Cambodia are among the most idiosyncratic of all south-east Asian pottery. The Neolithic pottery of Ban Chiang, painted in red pigment on a coarse buff ground, with semi-abstract designs has an international appeal. Later dark-brown glazed Khmer vessels are constructed in complex, architectural layers, and are truly individual.

While traditional pottery skills continue to be used in Japan, production in other Far Eastern centres now consists mainly of porcelain, celadon and *temmoku*, using modern techniques.

KOREAN CELADON

A moulded celadon bowl, some restoration, 12th/13thC; ht 7½in (19cm); value code F

Identification checklist for Korean celadon
1. Is the glaze irregular and/or dribbled?
2. Is it greyish-green and possibly crackled?
3. Are there three (or more) roughly circular marks left by the supports used in firing?
4. Does the glaze cover the base and footrim, apart from the spurs mentioned above?
5. Has the piece sagged or warped during firing?
6. Is the footrim neat and shallow (although occasionally wares are supported by a thin, slightly-splayed foot)?
7. Does the decoration feature flower motifs (other subjects are less common)?

The Koryu dynasty (935-1392 AD)
Celadon wares were introduced to Korea during the Koryu dynasty, and local potters were influenced by imports of Chinese Yue, Yaozhou and perhaps Ru wares. Production of unglazed stonewares continued, but celadon soon began to dominate the output.

Korean celadon
Depending on the firing conditions, the glaze on Korean celadon varies from a beautiful bluish-green, to a dull, olive-green or even a straw colour. The glaze is usually irregular and may be dribbled, and the surface of the glaze is occasionally crackled.
* Unglazed spur marks are commonly found on the feet of Korean celadon wares; there are usually three (sometimes more) of these.
* These spur marks can be fairly gritty and prominent, measuring as much as ¼in (0.6cm) in diameter, and are often as large as the spurs found on contemporary Jun ware (see pp. 32-3).

* Footrims are usually neat and shallow, although some wares, such as this cup stand from the 13thC, feature thin, slightly splayed feet.

Decoration
Many different types of decoration were used.
* Moulding or stamping: designs are dense, and commonly feature scrolling foliage. The bowl in the main picture has been finely moulded with an unusual design of double cranes with scrolling lotus leaves. The floral subjects on Korean celadon are similar to those found on northern Yaozhou celadon.

Made during the 13thC this pear-shaped vase with four floral sprigs and a band at the base of the neck, has been inlaid with black and white slip.

Types of wares
Vessels and dishes from this period include: bowls, footed dishes, bubble cups, small, straight-sided deep dishes, cosmetic boxes, wine cups and stands, oil jars, pear-shaped bottles, long-necked globular bottles or flasks, melon or bamboo-shoot shaped ewers and *meiping*.
* Decorated with white slip in the *mishima* style, the piece below is an oil jar or a water pot.

This lobed celadon bowl has been moulded with a large peony flower, an extremely popular motif.
* Carving: especially on the outside of vessels, included mainly floral or leaf subjects; wide, overlapping lotus petals are common.
* Incising: along with floral and leaf designs, other incised subjects include the phoenix, parrots and fish.

Inlaid wares
Inlaid or *mishima* wares were introduced in the middle of the 12thC. Here, an incised design is filled with coloured clays, covered with celadon glaze and fired.
* Decoration on early *mishima* wares included cranes, flowers and florets, usually in a formal arrangement.

Inlaid Punch'ong wares
An inlaid technique similar to *mishima* was used on later Punch'ong ware (made early 15th-late 16thC), using a material similar to celadon, but of an inferior quality. The designs were stamped onto the body which was then washed over in white slip and then wiped off. This technique leaves a less precise design than found on Koryu celadon.

KOREAN STONEWARE

An early stoneware vessel, c.200 BC;
ht 8¾in (22cm); value code F

Identification checklist for 5th-6thC Korean stoneware
1. Is the material dark grey?
2. Is the piece unglazed, or only slightly glazed on the upper surfaces, such as the shoulders?
3. If there is any decoration, does it feature small repeated motifs, such as dashes or circlets?
4. Is the object obviously distorted?

Early Korean pottery
Early Korean pottery is characterized by unglazed stoneware, made from a dark-bodied material with buff inclusions.
* The globular jar in the main picture has been paddle-beaten with an overall pattern that is probably intended to suggest basketweave.
* In spite of its very basic form, this jar has been wheel-turned.
* As with many antiquities, the prices of these wares are relatively low.

Types of wares
The range of wares produced includes covered funerary bowls, pedestalled vessels, oil lamps, food vessels and drinking cups.
Made in the 5th or 6thC the funerary jar and stand, right), is a good example of the architectural forms favoured by Korean potters

for this sort of vessel. Once again the decoration comprises small repeated motifs, in this case dashes, and incised bands.
* The spots on the shoulder of

the piece (below left) are caused by wood ash rising from the fire, settling on the pot during firing, and forming a treacly glaze.
* The triangular aperture in the stand is a regular feature of this form of ware.

Also from the 6thC, this piece also has an unusual architectural form. The decoration on the shoulders features a characteristic design of incised wavy lines and small circles.

Cizhou-style wares
Some Korean stonewares were made in the style of Chinese Cizhou wares (see pp.30-31). The Korean *meiping* below, c.12th-13thC, decorated with scrolling peony, has clearly been inspired by Cizhou wares.

The shape of the *meiping* (below left) is slightly squatter than the Chinese original on which it is based.
* Cizhou-style wares combine underglaze iron-brown with scratched details, and first appeared at the beginnning of the 12thC.

Hakeme glaze
Some later Korean stonewares known as Punch'ong wares, are decorated with *hakeme* ("brush-marked") glaze, where white or grey slip is brushed over the sur-face of the vessel.

Using a fine brush made from rice straw, the body of this *hakeme*-treated jar from the 15thC has been informally decorated with underglaze-brown, a colour used extensively in Korean pottery.
* *Hakeme* is intended to resemble field of corn or grasses being blown by the wind.
* The individuality of pieces such as this bowl, makes them extremely popular with the Japanese for use in the tea ceremony (see pp.40-1).
* *Hakeme* ware has been copied by Japanese potters right up to the present day, and Studio potters Bernard Leach and Shoji Hamada both employed the technique.

Collecting
Within the past decade there has been a great deal of interest in the field of Korean ceramics. Prices have generally tended to increase, even for primitive 18thC and late 19thC pieces, that until recently were not widely sought after. However, early stonewares have not attracted so much attention, and can be acquired relatively inexpensively: a good way to start a very interesting collection.

JAPANESE POTTERY

*An ovoid Satsuma earthenware jar, Meji period;
ht 7⅛in (18cm); value code E*

**An identification checklist for Japanese pottery would
be inappropriate because of the variety of forms,
styles and materials used.**

Japanese pottery

Japan has one of the longest
traditions in ceramics with
Neolithic wares that represent
some of the earliest dateable
pottery. While Japanese wares
were often loosely based on
Chinese or Korean pottery,
especially after the Middle
Ages, original Japanese forms
and styles were also produced.
* The sheer number of kilns
and individual potters in Japan,
who made all types of wares
based on forms and styles from
various regions and periods,
make attributions difficult,
although research and excavation
have now offered some clues.
* Until recently, many erroneous

attributions were made on the
basis of the Morse collection of
what was originally believed to
be early Japanese pottery,
assembled at the end of the
19thC, and now at the Museum
of Fine Arts, Boston.

The "Six Ancient Kilns"

The best and most influential
wares were made at the "Six
Ancient Kilns": Echizen,
Tamba, Tokoname, Bizen, Seto
and Shigaraki. Each of these
classic kilns (in fact they were
groups of kilns) produced
characteristic wares, which have
inspired hundreds of imitations
in different countries throughout
the following centuries.

Used for storing fresh water during the Tea Ceremony, this storage jar from Bizen (below), has been made in a strong form that exhibits the qualities that are demanded.

Produced in one of the group of kilns situated in the area known as Shigaraki, south of Kyoto, this storage jar is a fine example of the informality of the finest Japanese wares.
* Hand-coiled from local red clay, the surface has been smoothed and covered in a greyish, olive-green, wood-ash glaze in a typical manner.

The Tea Ceremony
Probably the most important or sought-after wares are those intended for the tea ceremony. The origins of this ceremony are found in China when Chan Buddhist monks used tea as a stimulant to keep themselves awake during long periods of meditation. Introduced to Japan in the 13thC, by the 15thC it had become a formal and exclusive rite, used by government officials, samurai and the nobility as a form of relaxation.

In the early years of the ceremony a combination of imported and Japanese ceramics would have been used, but by the 16thC native potters were encouraged to make wares specifically for the ceremony which displayed the "correct" qualities: *wabi* (austerity) and *sabi* (patina).

The idiosyncratic nature of these wares makes them difficult to attribute, but many were made at potteries such as Shino, Oribe, Seto, Karatsu and Bizen.

There are a number of vessels used during the tea ceremony; a tea bowl (*chawan*), that the host would expect the guest to examine and admire; a tea caddy (*chaire*), a small jar, often with a later ivory cover; a small dish (*mukozuke*) to hold the simple meal eaten during the ceremony, and a large jar (*mizusashi*) for holding water.

17thC wares
From the 17thC onwards, wares were enamelled with increasing complexity. In the Meji period (1868-1911), the kilns at Satsuma and Kyoto made elaborate, highly-coloured wares, that were popular in Europe at the end of the 19thC.
* The vase in the main picture is a good example of late enamelled earthenware, painted with a conventional Satsuma palette.
* A fine piece, this example is fully inscribed on the base, as were most high quality wares made at this time.
* Inscriptions or marks are very rare on pottery before the Meiji period.

A sensitively-painted piece, this Yabu Meizan earthenware dish from the Meiji period has been extensively gilded which is usual on these late wares intended for the export market.
* Snow scenes such as this one, were very popular in Europe during the 19thC.

OTHER CENTRES

*A guan-shaped wine jar, Northern Annam, mid-15thC;
ht 14in (35.5cm); value code D*

Identification checklist for Annamese wares
1. Does the piece have a low-shine glaze?
2. Does the glaze have a greyish/buff appearance?
3. Is the body close-grained and greyish?
4. Is the decoration complex?
5. Does the decoration feature panelled sections and floral motifs?
6. Is there a geometric border?
7. Is the piece monochrome?

Annamese pottery
Annam (present-day Vietnam) was active as a pottery-producing centre from the 13thC. Annamese ware is a type of stoneware/porcelain, with a close-grained greyish body. Decorated in monochrome, they are covered in a low-shine glaze which gives a greyish buff appearance.
* Pieces invariably have unglazed bases, but some are covered in a chocolate-brown wash, probably intended to imitate contemporary Chinese wares.

Types of wares
Invariably made in a compressed, globular form, Annamese wares are mainly small-scale (2-3in, 5-7.5cm), and include water droppers (round or animal-shaped – for example, toads), oil jars, bowls, *kendi* (a globular-shaped drinking vessel with a short spout), pear-shaped bottles and saucer dishes.
* Larger pieces tend to be based on Chinese forms, or are saucer dishes with lipped rims.
* Figures are very rare.

Smaller and less elaborate than the piece in the main picture, this vase is consequently much more affordable.

Decoration
The decoration on Annamese wares is characterized by its complexity. The panels seen both in the main picture and on the vase above are typical, and are based on decoration found on 14thC Yuan Chinese wares. Other characteristics are:
* geometric borders
* floral motifs, especially the lotus flower and peony.

Blue and white wares
Annamese potters produced a number of blue and white wares decorated with cobalt blue. Lower quality pieces were decorated using a native cobalt which produced a greyish colour with darker areas, while the finest wares were painted with bright blue, imported cobalt.
* Finely-painted with bright-blue cobalt, the bowl (right) was made in the 15thC.
* Many blue and white wares were made for export to South East Asia.

Thailand
There were two main kiln sites in Thailand, at Sawankhalok and Sukothai. They produced celadons, brownwares and painted wares (no underglaze blue). Thai pottery is made from a heavily grogged, gritty, dark grey material that looks peppered.

Types of wares
* Bowls, dishes, pear-shaped bottles, oil jars, small seated figures (made for religious purposes, their head were often knocked off for ritual purposes).
* Celadons were made mainly in Chinese forms: saucer dishes, compressed globular, fluted jars. The glaze is translucent, and it is possible to see right through to the body underneath.

Decoration
Thai pottery mainly features Chinese-style patterns divided into panels, as seen on 14thC Chinese blue and white wares. Painting is crude, and the brush-work is thick and unskilled.
* Whereas the Chinese original was generally decorated in under-glaze blue, Thai Sawankhalok and Sukothai wares are painted in a dark iron-brown, in a looser style.
* Iron brown does not usually allow the fine detailing achieved using cobalt blue.

Khmer pottery
Khmer pottery was made in the area that is now Cambodia, and consists of brownwares with some pale-green glazed wares. Pieces are characterized by sharp con-tours, incised geometric patterns, and stepped shoulders. Wares mainly oil jars, water droppers, bottles and dishes.

The brownware honey pot and cover (see left) from the 12thC features typical decoration, and a sharp, conical-shaped knop.
* Other pots were made in the form of animals (rabbits, elephants). In spite of their age, these are relatively inexpensive, and can form an interesting collection.

ISLAMIC POTTERY

A large Iznik blue and white pottery jug, mid-16thC

Islam as a religion was founded by the prophet Muhammed (AD c.570-632), whose revelations and teachings appear in the Islamic holy book, The Koran. From its establishment in the early 7thC, the culture of Islam spread quickly during the next 100 years, from its base in the Arabian peninsula to the Atlantic rim in the West, and to Samarkand and the Indus valley in the East. During this period the Islamic world was a centre for both learning and the decorative arts.

Islamic pottery has one of the richest and most diverse traditions in international ceramics, equal to that of China, although it fell short of the latter's supreme achievement, namely porcelain. Many of the important developments and techniques, familiar to the modern potter are of Islamic origin. Lustre ware, tin-glazing, fritware and underglaze blue decoration were either developed or refined in the Near and Middle East under Islam.

Chronologically, Islamic pottery can be broken down into three main periods: the early medieval period 622-1200 AD; the middle period 1200-1400; and the late or post-medieval period from 1400 onwards. This chapter deals with each of these periods using a non-geographical approach, necessary because of the diverse nature of the centres of production. Each of these areas produced wares, which, while conforming to general Islamic tradition, display local identifiable elements in material, potting, form, colour or style. For example, potters from Rayy (Rhages) and Kashan in Persia painted relatively large-scale figure and animal subjects in copper lustre. While similar in style and decoration, a closer inspection reveals a subtle difference in the treatment of the background.

In the first phase, the wares of Mesopotamia, Samarkand and Egypt rely on bold floral or geometric patterns and more rarely large-scale stylized images birds, animals or humans. In Nishapur in eastern Persia, the pottery painter felt confident enough to leave much of the surface bare of decoration, simply embellishing the rim of a dish with an inscription from the Koran or some abstract motif. Also in this early period, the influence of Tang wares is seen on the coloured lead-glazed pottery, and on some early white wares excavated at Samarra in the Persian Gulf, found alongside the Chinese porcelain objects on which they were based.

During the second period, again the influence of Song China is visible, especially in the 13thC. Here it was the white porcelains of Yingqing and Dingyao and the green celadons, particularly of Zhejiang that were copied by Islamic potters. But this interest in Chinese ceramics should not be allowed to create the impression that much of what was produced was merely imitative – these interactions encouraged Islamic potters to improve their craft technically, while retaining a distinctive decorative style.

In the post-medieval phase Near and Middle-Eastern potters were strongly influenced by China; this time by the blue and white porcelains of the Yuan and Ming dynasties. Some of the finest interpretations of early Ming blue and white were carried out by Turkish potters in the 16thC in Iznik and later Kütahya. In these two towns potters created the brilliant tiles which were incorporated into mosques and other important buildings. Painted with designs based on native vegetation – tulips, carnations, roses, cypress and a long saw-edged leaf, called *saz* in Turkish – they represent the best in later Islamic pottery. Their appeal was not confined to the Middle East, their influence can be seen on Italian maiolica from Padua in the 17thC, in France in the late 19thC, and in the work of William De Morgan in England, also in the late 19thC.

Also in the later period, the potters of Meshed and Kirman made thousands of copies of Chinese export blue and white wares which are very close, but can be distinguished by the composition of the body and the brushwork, although in some cases this can be difficult. These wares show little originality in their decoration, probably in response to the demands of the market. Some unscrupulous Dutch merchants passed off these Ming style fritwares as the real thing to an eager public in Holland. While such copies are surprisingly good, their similarity to the originals perhaps suggests aesthetic bankruptcy, or an indifference to the development of indigenous styles. Most late Persian pottery is either unexciting or derivative.

ISLAMIC CENTRES

This map identifies a number of important pottery-producing centres in the Islamic world during the three main periods of production.

In the first period, 622-1200 AD, the main centres were

Mesopotamia, a fertile region situated between two rivers, the Tigris and the Euphrates, Samarkand, Egypt, Samarra and Nishapur.

The second period, 1200-1400, was dominated by the refined

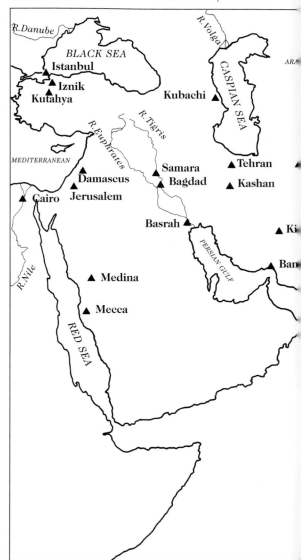

Persian wares of Kashan and Rayy, in present day Iran. These areas produced characteristic lustre wares, turquoise glazed wares, and enamelled "Minai" pottery.

Later Persian wares, from 1400 onwards, were produced in the south (Kirman), east (Meshed), and north of the country.

From the 15th-18thC, most Turkish pottery was produced in kilns in and around Iznik, about 60 miles (96.5km) from Istanbul. When production ceased at the beginning of the 18thC, a large proportion of Turkish pottery was made at Kütahya.

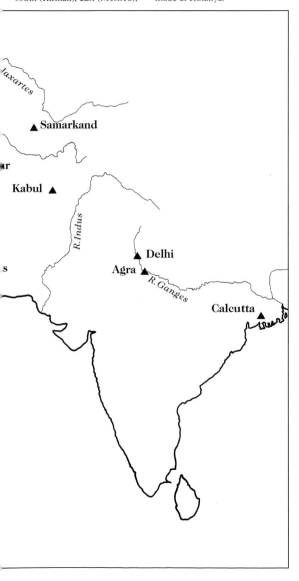

MESOPOTAMIAN POTTERY

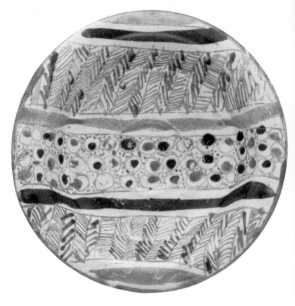

A small Mesopotamian lustre pottery dish, 9thC; ht 5⅜in (13.5cm); value code G

Identification checklist for 9thC Mesopotamian lustre wares
1. Is the item a piece of flatware (other forms are very unusual)?
2. Is the body made from fine, pale, straw-coloured material?
3. Is the piece thinly potted?
4. Does the piece feature more than one lustre colour?
5. If the piece has been decorated with copper lustre, is it a soft, brownish colour?
6. Does the decoration feature an abstract or vegetal design?

Mesopotamian pottery
Situated between the rivers Tigris and Euphrates in an area that is now Iraq, Mesopotamia was the site of two major technical developments in ceramics: the manufacture of high quality tin-glazed earthenware, and lustre decoration.
* The lustre technique was probably introduced from Egypt where glassmakers developed the technique.

Chinese influence
In the 9thC, Mesopotamian potters, who had been producing crude, local wares, were inspired by the arrival of Chinese ceramics (Tang, lead-glazed wares, greenwares and early white wares), which prompted a change in style and techniques. These reached the region by sea, and via the "Silk Route", running east over land from the Mediterranean to northern metropolitan China.

Made in the 9th or 10thC, this early Mesopotamian bowl illustrates the fusion of Islamic and Chinese styles that was occurring at this time. The form is based on a Chinese stoneware original, but the six-pointed star is an Islamic design.

This small, tin-glazed dish is based on a Tang form of which a number of examples have been excavated in Nishapur and other Islamic sites. The tentative splashed decoration is also reminiscent of southern Chinese stoneware, however the *kufic* inscription which reads "amal salih" ("the work of Salih") is characteristic of this early group.
* Here the painter has used cobalt blue and copper green, a common combination, although blue alone was also popular. Other colours employed on this type were manganese brown and quite rarely, yellow.
* Notice how the green stripes have blurred by being partly absorbed into the yellowish-creamy glaze, a typical flaw.

Categories
There are several categories of Mesopotamian pottery:
* low-fired, unglazed pale-bodied wares decorated by moulding,

scratching, applying or painting,
* lead-glazed wares decorated in relief with a wide range of local and foreign designs,
* lead-glazed, red-bodied wares, with scratched (*sgraffiato*) designs,
* lustre wares.

Lustre wares
Lustred pottery was a cheap substitute for more precious objects, such as gold or silver, which were in an abundant supply places such as the Abbasid court (the Abbasids led the Islamic world from 749-1258 AD). With their ostentatious style, lustre wares have a direct appeal.
* The warm white glaze on the piece in the main picture is painted in yellow and ruby lustre, although an olive-brown, plain brown, and a silvery green were also available at this time.
* Early lustre colours included ruby, brown, yellow, black and a plain red. By the mid-9thC two colours appeared, usually brown and yellow.
* During the 10thC polychrome lustre was abandoned in favour of a single colour per piece.

Abstract designs are found on ceramics throughout the Islamic world, but on this shallow lustre bowl from the 9th-10thC, the use of wedge-shaped dashes, together with the "frogspawn" or pheasant's eye pattern are typical of Iraq.
* The two-coloured lustre is also a characteristic of this area.

Marks
Mesopotamian wares do not bear factory or workshop marks, but a few pieces are signed by individuals.
* A useful guide to authenticity is wear: look for natural wear on the footrim.

EARLY PERSIAN WARES

*A Kashan copper lustre, bird-headed ewer, early 13thC;
ht 9¾in (24.7cm); value code C*

Identification checklist for 12th-13thC Kashan lustre wares
1. Is the body made from fine pinkish or greyish-buff material?
2. Is the clay peppered with tiny flecks?
3. Is the piece thinly-potted?
4. Has the body been covered with off-white slip?
5. Is the glaze crackled?
6. Does the surface feature an iridescent sheen?
7. Is the body exposed at the foot of the piece?
8. If the piece is painted with copper lustre, is the colour vivid?
9. Does the decoration feature a calligraphic design?

Early Persian pottery
From the beginning of the 11thC the Seljuk Turks controlled much of western Asia (with the exception of Syria). Persia (now Iran) and the other countries under Seljuk rule underwent a period of great cultural development. The pottery produced at this time at the great centres of Rayy and Kashan, probably helped by Egyptian expertise, are among the most refined of all Islamic wares.

Characteristics

Generally Persian pottery is made from fine pinkish or greyish-buff clay, peppered with tiny flecks. It is thinly potted and covered in an off-white slip, which runs down to the foot of the piece with a curtain-like effect, leaving the body partly exposed. The glaze covering the slip is usually crackled. Because of the porous nature of the body, most pieces have become a dirty tan or brown colour.

Kashan wares

Plain and lustred pottery was made in Kashan, south of Teheran, between 1215 and 1334. The majority of wares were bowls, but a number of more ambitious forms were also produced, based on glass or silver forms.
* In contrast to the bowl, below, the ewer in the main picture has a more elaborate form. The cockerel's head is a familiar motif in Persian pottery.

In extremely good condition, this bowl from the early 13thC, has a characteristic Persian form that is ridged or "carinated" above a tall foot.
* The dark, vivid colour of the copper lustre on this bowl is typical of Kashan.
* The production of lustre wares in Persia began in the 12thC. The technique was probably brought to the area by Egyptian potters following the collapse of the Fatimid dynasty in 1171.

Turquoise wares

As well as lustre wares, pottery covered with a rich, vivid, turquoise glaze was also made in Kashan.

Made in the 12th/13thC, the small ewer (4½ in, 11cm) above, shows clearly how the thick glaze runs down the sides of the piece during firing, forming an irregular line around the foot.
* Due to a long period of burial, many turquoise-glazed pieces show signs of breakdown in the glaze, leaving an iridescent sheen on the surface.
* Turquoise glaze was also used over pieces painted with black designs, and over moulded or engraved decoration.

Decoration

* Many Persian wares are decorated with calligraphic foliage and vines. Simple, repetitive designs, such as the "circle and dot" pattern on the lustre bowl above left, were also used.
* Influenced by Fatimid motifs, Persian pottery in the middle of the 12thC often featured large, bold human figures (as seen on the piece in the main picture). By the 13thC figures became smaller and less significant (see the "Minai" bowl below).

"Minai" wares

Made in Rayy near Teheran, "Minai" wares were painted with pale blue, green or light purple designs under a cream glaze, these were outlined in black, and a wide range of enamel colours were added over the glaze. Some pieces also feature gilding.
* Painted with two musicians around a tree inside a detailed border, this "Minai" bowl was made in the 13thC.

LATER PERSIAN WARES

*One of a pair of Safavid blue and white pottery bottles
c.17th-18thC; ht 18 ¾in (47.5cm); value code C*

Identification checklist for 17th-18thC Safavid blue
and white wares
1. Does the underglaze blue appear runny?
2. Has the brushwork been executed in a calligraphic
style?
3. Does the design appear to be an Islamic
interpretation of Chinese blue and white decoration?
4. Does the design include drooping foliage?
5. Is the glaze thick and glassy?
6. Is the footrim a brownish colour?
7. Is the glazed surface crackled?
8. Are there pinholes in the glaze?

Later Persian pottery
During the Safavid and later
periods, Persian potters
produced a considerable
amount of material, both for the
domestic market, and for export
to Mogul India and even Europe,
where records show that some
merchants tried to pretend
that they were selling genuine
Chinese porcelain. Some of
the Persian blue and white
wares are very accurate copies
of Chinese pieces.

* The bottle in the main picture is a good example of Persian blue and white pottery. It features a clearly Islamic-style interpretation of Chinese blue and white decoration, with drooping foliage painted with calligraphic brushwork.
* The discoloured footrim, and crackled glaze are characteristic of Safavid wares.

Chinese influence

Most later Persian wares are very close to their Chinese prototypes, but some styles are easier to identify and have their own names, including "Kubachi", "Meshed" and "Kirman".
* Meshed (east Persian) and Kirman (south Persian) wares are similar in material, form and style: white frit paste, thick, soft glaze and flowing, calligraphic brushwork. It is very difficult to distinguish between the two, although some experts believe that black outlining around the designs indicates a Meshed piece.

Based on a Chinese original, this large 17thC plate has been decorated in the style of 16thC Chinese porcelain from the Jiajing period (1522-66), with an inner ring. But the design itself, particularly the flowers and leaves, is clearly Persian.

Kubachi wares

Made in northern Persia, most Kubachi wares in existence today are dishes, either plain or barbed, in the style of Chinese blue and white Ming porcelain. Designs tend to follow the Chinese, but some have a strong native Persian, or occasionally Turkish feel. In the latter case many are painted with bold, formal flowers and saw-edged leaves found on "Rhodian" Iznik wares.

Colours

Polychrome Persian wares include the following colours.
* Pre-1550: black, deep blue, purple, turquoise, red, ochre.
* Post-1550: black, smudgy, deep blue, turquoise, dull green, yellow-ochre, and a brown-red not unlike that derived from "Armenian bole" (see p.57).

As seen on the Kubachi bowl above, from the 16thC, the palette of later Persian wares resembles the later "Rhodian" Iznik ware, and to some extent Kütahya ware (see pp.54-5 and pp.56-7).
* Occasionally the surface of the vessel is covered entirely in ochre, or soft salmon-pink, and then painted over in the usual style.
* A small group of wares were painted in black under a turquoise or green glaze.

"Gombroon" wares

Made from fine, white fritware, that is cut through with tiny "windows" and then filled with a transparent glaze, "Gombroon" wares were intended to imitate decoration found on some types of porcelain.

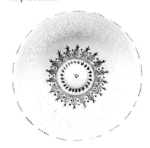

Named after the port of Bandar Abbas in the Persian Gulf (formerly known as Gombroon), the embellishment on wares such as the bowl above, c.17thC, is termed "rice grain" decoration.

53

TURKEY: IZNIK

*An Iznik blue-and-white pottery candlestick, c.1480;
ht 9in (25cm); value code B*

Identification checklist for 16thC Turkis Iznik wares
1. Does the piece have a greyish-buff body?
2. Is the footrim neat and cut straight across?
3. Does the base have a kiln support mark (a small, unglazed, circular blemish) in the centre?
4. Is the glaze smooth with a blue tint where thick?
5. Does the design feature flowers and other vegetation (especially "saw-edged" leaves)?

Iznik wares
Until recently our understanding of Turkish pottery made under Ottoman rule from the 15th-19thC has been confused by a lack of information. A scheme of classification introduced in the 19thC gave names to particular styles (such as "Miletus", "Damascus" and "Rhodian" ware). However, research has shown that all these wares were made at the same kilns at Iznik, about 60 miles (96.5km) east of

Istanbul, but the terms are still of use when describing different decorative styles.

Early wares
Made in the late 14th and 15thC, "Miletus" wares have a red body, covered in slip, painted in dark cobalt, turquoise, and sometimes black. The decoration usually comprises geometric patterns and stylized vegetation. Some feature Chinese-style motifs or flowers.

Material

The composition of the body of Iznik wares is of a greyish/buff clay with a grainy, absorbent-looking surface. It is covered in a translucent, quite glassy glaze, mostly of uniform thickness, but where it does pool or gather in corners it has a definite bluish tone. The clay appears to allow large scale potting without much sign of sagging or distortion.

* The base is usually flat with a slight bulge in the centre, visible on the front, caused by the small circular stilt used in the firing.

A number of large 16thC dishes, based on Chinese porcelain pieces have survived, that demonstrate the plasticity and strength, as well as the refinement, of the clay used at Iznik. The decoration on this example from the first half of the 16thC shows a clear Chinese influence.

* Based on an early 15thC original, the design represents clusters of grapes, a popular motif. The wave pattern on the rim is also derivative.

Styles

Some styles of Iznik pottery are so distinctive that they have been named.

* The "Abraham of Kutahya" style, c.1490-1520: Italianate forms (eg. bell-shaped candlesticks) decorated with entwined foliage and flower heads, often white on a blue ground. The name is from an inscribed ewer, dated 1510.

* "Golden Horn" wares, c.1530: excavated on the Golden Horn in Istanbul, decorated with pencilled scrolls resembling circles of barbed wire. Mainly underglaze blue, some with turquoise and manganese purple.

* "Damascus" ware, c.1550-70:

among the most sumptuous of all Islamic pottery. Painted in a wide range of colours, including mushroom, sage-green, turquoise, a soft and a dark blue and black. Large-scale, floral subjects, and characteristic saw-edged leaves (*saz*).

* "Rhodian" wares, c.1555-1700: palette extended to include a rich copper green and a strong orange-red, known as "sealing-wax red", seen here on this dish from the second half of the 16thC. Decoration is mainly floral subjects (tulip, carnation, rose and hyacinth, which tend to issue from one point on the surface), but occasionally ships and more rarely figures are found. Some geometric and abstract foliate motifs also appear. Flatwares have a scroll-pattern border.

Made in the late 16thC, this simple cylindrical-shaped piece with an angular handle is the most popular form of Iznik tankard. It features a tulip with a small, basket-weave border, another popular motif.

Marks

A handful of pieces are inscribed and dated, generally with dedicatory inscriptions.

Six Kütahya pottery dishes, mid-18thC;
dia. 5-6in (12.7-15.2cm); value code D/E

Identification checklist for 18thC Kütahya wares
1. Does the piece have a buff-coloured body?
2. Is it thinly-potted?
3. Is the piece an item of tableware (other types are less common)?
4. Does the piece measure 4-8in (10.2-20.3cm)?
5. Does the decoration include crude floral or figural subjects?
6. Is the glaze irregular, with greenish or bluish areas?
7. Does the palette include black, manganese, copper-green, brown-red, cobalt and particularly ochre?

17thC Turkish pottery
During the 17thC there was a marked decline in both technical and decorative skills at the Iznik kilns, and in c.1700 the potteries ceased production entirely. After this date, a large number of distinctive pottery wares were made at Kütahya in central Anatolia.

Kütahya

Situated further inland than Iznik, Kütahya is particularly noted for its 18thC wares, although some potteries were clearly in production long before this date, even perhaps as early as the 15thC. Indeed, some of the first wares to be made in Kütahya have been confused with pieces from Iznik.

Characteristics

18thC Kütahya wares are characterized by a buff-coloured, thinly-potted body, covered with an irregular glaze which pools into greenish or bluish areas.
* The decoration on pieces from Kütahya is crude, and subjects are usually floral or figural, as seen on the dishes in the main picture.
* These dishes also challenge the popularly-held belief that Islamic law forbade the depiction of the human form. These men and women are wearing contemporary 18thC Turkish costume.

Collecting

Although Turkish pottery, especially early Iznik wares are highly sought after, it is possible to collect less sophisticated, but highly attractive 17thC pieces for relatively small sums.

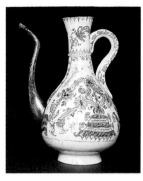

A rare item made c.1745, this pear-shaped ewer is based on a classic Chinese shape, a form first produced in Kütahya in the early 18thC. Larger than usual (11¼ in, 28.8cm), this piece features relatively dense decoration.

Colours

Usually polychrome, colours found on wares from Kütahya include black, manganese, copper green, brown-red, cobalt and ochre.
* The red glaze on Kütahya wares is derived from the same source as Iznik "sealing wax" red, a bright-red clay coloured by iron oxide, known as Armenian bole.

Tablewares

Small vessels for the table make up the major portion of the output at Kütahya, including dishes, bowls, mugs, coffee pots and ewers, such as the pieces showns below. This group of later wares, from the first half of the 18thC, measure 4-8in (10.2-20.3cm) in height.
* Note the tight patterns typical of later Kütahya wares, and also the use of yellow which does not appear on Iznik pottery.

SPANISH &
PORTUGUESE POTTERY

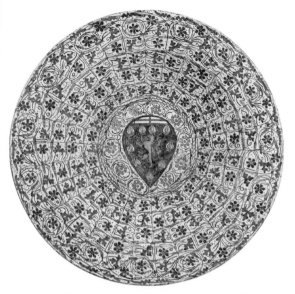

An Hispano-moresque lustred pottery armorial dish, c.1450

Spain plays an important role in the history of European pottery: that of elevating a utilitarian material into a respected decorative art form. The Moorish conquest of Spain brought a considerable number of benefits, the skills of the potter among them. Lustred tin-glaze had been developed in Egypt and Mesopotamia, probably in the 9thC. The technique spread throughout the Middle East, reaching southern Spain probably in the 12thC. In all likelihood the craft in Spain was given a considerable boost by the arrival of Fatimid potters (an Islamic sect powerful in the Middle East during the 10th and early 11thC) from Egypt escaping from the fall of their dynasty in 1171 AD. Later the Mongolian invasion of Persia and Syria encouraged another wave of potters anxious to follow their trade in the more sympathetic environment of Spain.

An Arabic geographer, Muhammad ibn-Muhammad writing in the middle of the 12thC speaks of "gold coloured pottery" which was then being exported from Calatayud in Aragon. Other Arabic writers from around 1300 praise the golden ware of Malaga and remark on its popularity abroad. In 1289 a gift of Malaga pottery for Queen Eleanor of Castile, the first wife of Edward I, arrived at Portsmouth and included "42 bowls, 10 dishes, 4 earthenware jars of foreign colour". Another early reference from 1303 informs us that "30 bowls and pitchers of Malyk (Malaga)" were imported at the port of Sandwich. These and other references are among the very earliest to European ceramics available and however slight they appear they give some indication that they were noteworthy items, not simply common objects.

By the 15thC Malaga had been supplanted by Valencia, aided by a steady stream of Malagan potters who had migrated to Catalonia from about 1350. It is sometimes extremely difficult to distinguish the wares from these two locations, particularly in the 14th and early 15thC. Valencian lustre wares began to appear in Netherlandish and Italian paintings by artists such as Hugo van der Goes and Filippino Lippi. Furthermore, pieces were commissioned by prominent Florentine families, many of whom had trading connections with Spain. A surprising number of these impressive armorial dishes and vessels have survived.

Perhaps it is because Italian maiolica progressed so quickly in the 15th and 16thC, that the market for Hispano-moresque pottery began to decline. The appeal of lustre ware lies in its naturally brilliant metallic surface but it is limited by being a "flat" type of decoration, relying on line and space. The Italian potter developed a broad range of colours which he soon learned to modulate and so create sophisticated graphic images and depth.

Valencia continued to produce pottery but it became increasingly mechanical and cursory in the 16th and 17thC. By this time other Spanish potteries had been established producing wares in the more fashionable narrative style. Puente del Arzobispo and Talavera made robust pieces, painted in a lively manner with equestrian figures, hunting scenes, bullfights and animals after engravings by Johannes Stradanus and his pupil Antonio Tempesta. King Philip III had given the potteries an unexpected boost in 1601 by restricting the use of silver due to its shortage. Pottery proved to be a successful substitute and it was not long before the noble families of Spain were eating off tin-glazed dishes. The output of these factories included not only dishes and vessels for the domestic market but considerable quantities of tiles and drug jars for the pharmacies attached to the hospitals of the various religious orders in Spain. The pottery of this period is painted mainly in green, ochre and blue, similar to the palette used by many Italian factories at this time. These wares enjoyed considerable international recognition in the 17thC.

In the 18thC the mantle of ceramic leadership passed to Alcora. French pottery painters were brought in to teach the local potters the current style of decoration. Many of the Alcora wares of the early to mid 18thC look similar to those of Moustiers and Marseilles. Alcora also produced porcelain, and, towards the end of the 18thC, *terra de pipa*, a pottery not unlike creamware. With the development of these two wares the production of high quality tin-glazed pottery had virtually stopped by the turn of the century. In the present day many of these traditional Spanish wares are copied and bear marks; early wares are rarely marked.

15TH & 16THC SPANISH POTTERY

*An Hispano-Moresque dish, Catalonia, early 16thC;
dia. 15in (38.1cm); value code G*

Identification checklist for 16thC Spanish lustre wares
1. Is the piece made from warm-looking, buff material?
2. Is the surface pinkish (with a slightly dirty appearance)?
3. Is the glaze irregular?
4. Are the designs relatively dense, perhaps including a small, repeating, geometric motif?
5. If a piece of flatware, has the rim been pierced with one or two holes where the piece was suspended during firing?
6. Is the lustre a copper-red colour?

Early Spanish pottery
A considerable body of material has survived from the early days of Spanish pottery production, including a number of tiles. Early wares produced by Moorish potters in the extreme south of Spain at Malaga and Seville show a strong Islamic influence.

Made c.1400, at Manises (Valencia), this early lustre dish shows how the Moorish influence spread northwards. The motifs are representations of the Islamic "Tree of Life", and "Alafia" character which conveys a benign wish or blessing.

* Manises wares are generally less precise than pieces that originate from Malaga.

Decorative motifs

Subjects found on Spanish lustre ware include animals such as lions, deer, bulls and goats. Decoration is usually relatively dense. By the late 15thC there is evidence that lustre wares were beginning to be mass-produced, and on many pieces small, repetitive patterns replace the fluent brushwork of the best earlier lustre wares.

* One of the most common motifs in 15th and 16thC lustre ware is bryony, a small floret comprising six dark dots with a paler centre.

Also from Manises, made during the early 16thC, this dish is decorated with typical small, repeating patterns and stylized foliage.

* The spiralling, moulded border based on a silver original was found on many dishes after c.1500.

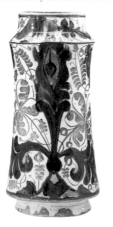

Italian-style, lustre ware albarelli were also made, such as this 15thC example from Manises.

Albarelli from this area are generally crisply-angled at the bases and shoulders, and as here, waisted on the upper third of the main body giving a tapered effect.

* On some albarelli, the neck can be almost twice as high as seen here, and may also have a more pronounced lip.

* A rare and valuable piece, the cobalt-blue *fleur-de-lys* decoration on this albarello is unusual, but the surrounding fern-like vegetation is characteristic of Valencian pottery.

* The pale-brownish tone of the lustre on this piece is standard on Spanish wares, although a more coppery red is also common, as seen on the dish in the main picture.

Armorial wares

Armorial lustre wares were made in Spain for both and home foreign consumption.

The arms that appear on this dish c.1475-1500 are similar to those of the Grimaldi family of Genoa, although this is not certain.

Dating

As early Spanish pottery is unmarked, many pieces can be attributed by comparing them with decoration on armorial wares made for individuals, particularly noblemen, for whom accurate dates can be given.

* The trefoils on the dish above, appear on many inscribed pieces, and allow the piece to be dated with reasonable assurance.

Collecting

Large numbers of Spanish lustre wares were produced until the 17thC in an attempt to compete with Italian, and later French faience. As a result, many pieces can be acquired for relatively modest sums.

17TH & 18THC SPANISH POTTERY

A tin glazed inkwell, Puento del Arzobispo or Talavera, 17thC;
wdth 7in (17.8cm); value code G

Identification checklist for 17thC tin-glazed wares
1. Is the piece made from a warm pinkish, biscuit-coloured material?
2. Does the palette include ochre, manganese, cobalt-blue, yellow and green?
3. Has manganese been used as an outline?
4. Is the glaze relatively thick?
5. If the decoration features foliage, does it look frothy?
6. Have the leaves been highlighted in green and ochre?

17th and 18thC Spanish pottery
While Spain is best-known for its lustre ware, in the 17th and 18thC there was a tendency to imitate foreign techniques and styles, such as the strong Italian maiolica palette in the 17thC, and the style of southern French faïence in the 18thC.

Puento del Arzobispo
Located near Toledo in central Spain, the workshop at Puento de Arzobispo made faïence during the 17thC. The most notable pieces are boldly painted in cobalt-blue and ochre, with animal and figure subjects surrounded by a loose frame of stylized vegetation.
* Wares from Puento del Arzobispo

are very similar to those of Talavera, but the former are characterized by a dull, pinkish surface, that is finely speckled with tiny, peppery dots.
* Many inkwells such as the piece in the main picture were made at Talavera and Puento del Arzobispo. This piece is painted in a palette that includes ochre, manganese and cobalt-blue. The feathery fronds are also typical.

Talavera de la Reina
Situated not far from Puento del Arzobispo, maiolica and faïence were first made in Talavera from the early part of the 16thC onwards. Wares are smooth-looking under a lead glaze.
* Many inkwells such as the piece in the main picture were

made at Talavera and Puento del Arzobispo.
* This piece is painted in a typical palette including ochre, manganese and cobalt-blue.

The leaning, frothy foliage found on wares from Talavera, seen here on this footed dish from the late 17thC, is immediately recognizable. The leaves tend to be heightened with yellow and ochre.

Many pieces from this period are painted with figurative themes, often with hunting scenes based on popular engravings.

Alcora (est.1727)
During the 18thC, the pottery at Alcora in Valencia produced highly refined wares in the French manner as a result of employing leading French potters from Moustiers and Marseilles. The factory made a variety of tableware and more decorative items.

Many wall plaques, such as the one here c.1760, were made at Alcora. Painted with soft enamels this piece has been painted in the rococo style fashionable in France during this period.

* Also found on wares from Alcora are grotesque designs, and fantastic animals and birds arranged between clumps of vegetation. Both these styles are based on decoration used at Moustiers.
* More ambitious pieces include portrait busts and centrepieces.
* By the end of the 18thC Alcora was producing a range of cream-coloured earthenwares, in an attempt to keep pace with the general fashion for this type of pottery in Europe.

Characteristics
* Made from pale greyish-pink clay, Alcora faience is covered in a waxy glaze which gives a greyish-green tone on most pieces.
* The colours used at Alcora include red, manganese, blue, yellow and a greyish-green.

Made in Catalonia in the north east of Spain, this Spanish albarello has a typical silhouette. The large-scale ornament, such as the thickly-painted scrolling foliage that resembles wrought iron on this piece, is characteristic of 17th and early 18thC pottery.

Marks
Apart from a few signatures, pre-18thC pottery is not marked. Some Alcora wares feature marks.

PORTUGUESE POTTERY

*A detail from the centre of a blue and white faïence dish, 17thC;
dia. 16in (40.6cm); value code E/F*

**Identification checklist for Portuguese blue and white
faïence**
1. Is the cobalt either pale and greyish or dark,
verging on black?
2. Does the decoration feature a compartmentalized
design that is based on late Ming porcelain?
3. Has the piece been painted in a relatively loose style?
4. Does the brushwork have a swirling motion?
5. Does the design appear as if it is almost melting?

Portuguese pottery
Portugal was one of the major
cultural bastions in post-Medieval
Europe with a strong tradition in
tin-glazed earthenwares. 16thC
faïence was made in an Italianate
style and is barely distinguishable
from other centres such as Faenza,
or from Netherlands maiolica.
* Pottery production in Portugal
was primarily for home consumption, although there is
evidence of a later export
industry (see *facing page*).

Chinese influence
The Portuguese had pioneered
the sea passage to China in the
early years of the 16thC, and
by Royal decree, merchants
were forced to bring back
thousands of pieces of Chinese
porcelain in the holds of their
large trading ships or carracks.
(Called *kraak* in the Netherlands,
the style of ceramics taken to
Holland by this type of craft
became known as *kraakporselein*
(see pp. 96-7).

By the 17thC, Portuguese
pottery was made predomi-
nantly in the Chinese style.
Produced in the mid-17thC,
this bulbous vase is an out-
standing example of
Portuguese blue and white
faïence. The compartmentalized
decoration is characteristic of
late Ming porcelain.
* Towards the end of the
17thC the Ming style became
very loose. The chrysanthemum
is a popular motif, and some
armorials were produced.

The Ming-style border on this 17thC blue and white dish from Lisbon, has been combined with the central figure of Fortuna, originally found on drugs jars from Castel Durante. Fortuna, the Roman Goddess of Fortune, was a popular subject with merchants.
* Lisbon faience painters used a greyish cobalt outlined with relatively thin manganese outlines.

Painting
Compared with the rigorous designs of the pottery decorators in Delft, the style of painting on Portuguese blue and white wares is much looser with swirling brushwork. Often it appear as if the design has partly melted.

Decorated once again with a Ming-style border, this dish features deer within a dense, forest scene.

Tiles
A large number of high quality tiles were produced in Portugal from the 16thC. Greatly influenced by Netherlandish tile decorators, some of the painting on early panels of tiles in Portuguese churches, has been attributed to Dutch artists.

Rato (1767-19thC)
In 1767 the Royal factory at Rato near Lisbon was founded by an Italian from Milan called Thomaz Brunetto. This factory produced baroque decorative wares and elaborate rococo tablewares.

A group of animal-shaped vessels were made at Rato, such as this goose-shaped tureen c.1750-70, Based on a Chinese *famille-rose* original, this one features the coat of arms of a Portuguese nobleman.

Types of wares
Dishes form the majority of the output, but other wares include ewers with snake handles, tall albarelli, baluster jars with an angular, ovoid shape, bottles and dishes.

In the 18thC forms became more elegant, elongated or curvaceous, and a wide range of tablewares were produced. A group of portrait busts and figures indicate that the Portuguese followed the influence of the general European trend for first the rococo and subsequently the Neo-classical styles.
* Some ewers are very similar to those made in Hamburg, Germany. This may be explained by close trading links between Portugal and a powerful group of German merchants based in Hamburg, known as the Hanseatic League.

Marks
Most Portuguese factories used marks, mainly simple initials such as the "F.R." of the Rato factory.
* Other 18thC Portuguese faience-producing centres include, Aeiro, Santo Antonio, Coimbra and Miragaya.

ITALIAN MAIOLICA

A Castel Durante maiolica dish, c.1515-20

Tin-glazed earthenware has been made in Italy since at least the 13thC, but it was not until the 15thC that it acquired a truly individual style. Following the lead of Spanish pottery developed during the 13th and 14thC, in the space of 100 years, Italian tin-glazed wares advanced from utilitarian copper-green and manganese-brown decorated wares, to sophisticated and complex painted masterpieces.

The term "maiolica" is probably derived from the old Tuscan word for the island of Majorca through which Hispano-moresque lustre wares were shipped to Italy in the 14th and 15thC. Originally the term would have applied solely to lustre ware, but not long after was used for all Italian tin-glazed pottery. Italian maiolica is classified by style and then, if possible, by region, town and workshop. Few pieces of maiolica are signed and no more than about a dozen potter-artists are known by their work.

The major output of the pottery industry was everyday wares. Once broken, they were discarded, and have been excavated from post-medieval rubbish pits. This early type of pottery, if decorated at all, is crudely painted in green and brown. Subjects include simple vegetation, birds or animals, often on a background decorated with fine lines (hatched or cross-hatched). Few, invariably damaged, specimens appear on the market and can be bought for relatively modest amounts. This group is termed archaic.

In the second half of the 15thC there was a marked advance in potting and decorative skill. More complicated designs, occasionally featuring figures, fit the contours of the dish or vessel in a highly structured way. Towards the end of the century, semi-narrative figure subjects, mostly of an allegorical or moralistic nature appear, although these are rare.

The arrival of the printed book and the diffusion of engravings provided a major source for the pottery artist. At the beginning of the 16thC engravings of the "grotesques" or grotto wall decorations from Nero's Golden House, discovered in c.1480, were widely copied. Grotesques are figures of men, fantastic creatures and winged cherubs that were usually used to create detailed borders for 16thC wares. They continued to be used throughout the next two centuries, but were adapted so that designs became more open, often featuring white highlighting, and the figures themselves became more muscular.

Printed sources also led to the most important development in Italian maiolica, namely the *istoriato* or narrative style. It was practised at all major maiolica centres: Faenza, Venice, Pesaro, Gubbio, and Urbino which is most closely associated with the *istoriato* style. Most of the legends or myths depicted on these wares are based on classical works. Figures and scenes from different sources were used by pottery painters to complete a story, that is usually "read" from left to right across the piece. Prominent artists are Nicola da Urbino and Francesco Xanto Avelli da Rovigo, who have signed a number of dishes, and more have been attributed to them. Other artists are known simply from their stylistic idiosyncrasies.

At the beginning of the 16thC *istoriato* pottery was painted in stiff, frieze-like compositions in a cool bluish palette. By about 1530 figures became livelier and were painted in warmer tones, with orange counterbalancing a clear sky blue. In the latter half of the century, designs in the mannerist style were used in most pottery centres.

The tradition of narrative pottery continued in different regions of Italy until the end of the 18thC, such as Siena and Castelli. Raphael and the old influences are replaced with more up-to-date images derived from artists such Antonio Tempesta and Aegidius Sadeler as well as contemporary pastoral scenes with overgrown classical buildings.

By no means all the maiolica made for the upper end of the market was *istoriato*; a considerable proportion was decorated with formal foliage or arabesques, trophies of war and music, strapwork and grotesques. Grotesque motifs became increasingly spindly in the second half of the century, very different from the three-dimensional versions found in early 15thC maiolica. Use of grotesque decoration continued well into the 17thC, and was adopted by French, Netherlandish and English potters.

Another popular style of decoration, *quartieri*, also travelled far from Italy, especially to Sicily and France. Here the piece is painted in a series of small, mainly floral, scroll panels, rather like a patchwork quilt. Toward the end of the 16thC Faentine potters began to paint in the *compendiario* style, using a yellow ochre and blue in an almost cursory manner with *putti* (cupids and cherubs) and casually-painted vegetation. Production of high quality pottery carried on in the 17th and 18thC, but by this time, potters in France and Holland had begun to produce new, more fashionable styles.

ITALIAN CENTRES

The first important maiolica-producing centres in Italy in the 15thC were Orvieto (possibly the oldest), Viterbo, Tuscany (Florence and Siena), and Faenza. Others include Rome, Padua, Cortona and Todi.

Many wares produced in the middle of the 15thC show a Spanish influence, particularly those made in Tuscany, but a native style began to develop, notably the polychrome wares made in Faenza from c.1470.

The production of maiolica was well-established by the beginning of the 16thC, and output included large dishes and sets of drug jars. An important centre during the 16thC, potters in Deruta made maiolica with large-scale, polychrome decoration, and also a group of golden and ruby lustre wares were produced c.1500-1550. These lustre wares are characterized by highlighting in cobalt-blue. Lustreing was later taken up by potters in Gubbio, most successfully by Maestro Giorgio Andreoli.

One of the most characteristic decorative styles, *isoriato* or pictorial painting was perfected in Castel Durante and Urbino during the first quarter of the 16thC. Here the artist uses the object as a canvas, on which to represent some narrative subject derived from biblical, allegorical, mythological or genre sources. The style was quickly taken up by pottery painters in other areas, and continued to be popular until the end of the 16thC. Also important at this time were Pesaro and Forlì, and some pottery was produced in Rimini and Verona.

Another decorative form developed in and around Urbino during the 16thC, was the grotesque. This was a fantastical type of ornament, originally based on the wall decoration of the underground ruins of Emperor Nero's Golden House, which was rediscovered in 1480. The painter Raphael and his assistants incorporated these themes into the decoration of the Vatican *Loggie* in 1518-19. They include a wide variety of half-human beasts, masks, scrollwork and threads arranged in a number of different ways.

A style of decoration characteristic of pottery made in Faenza at about this time is called *compendiario*, Here the palette consisted mainly of blue, detailed in yellow and ochre, and the painting was usually executed with a free, unlaboured hand.

In the 17th and early 18thC, the maiolica tradition continued with some high quality pieces made at Venice and Castelli, while coarser, more primitive wares made at centres in Sicily such as Palermo and Caltagirone.

While a number of factories are still in operation today, the Chinese influence beginning in the 17thC, changed the nature of the output of many Italian centres, with imitations of Dutch Delft, and later French faience.

EARLY ITALIAN MAIOLICA

A Florentine double-handled drug jar, c.1430;
ht 12in (20.5cm); value code A/B

Identification checklist for early Italian maiolica
1. Does the piece have a brownish or buff-coloured clay body?
2. Is the glaze a dirty off-white?
3. Does the piece have brown and green decoration?
4. If so, is the brown used as an outline only, and the green used as a wash only?
5. Is the decoration primitive and clumsily executed?
6. Is the brushwork thickly drawn?
7. Is the subject floral or animal?
8. Is the object heavily (ie. thickly) potted?
9. If there is blue, has it been applied as a flat, greyish wash or is it thicker with the apparent consistency of jam?

Early wares

The earliest documented European pottery is a large group of drug jars commissioned for the Ospedale della Santa Maria Nuova in Florence from the workshop of Giunta di Tugio in 1430-31. These drug jars are marked with the device of the hospital, a crutch, and are usually thickly painted in blackish cobalt blue with different motifs on a ground of stylized oak leaves, as seen on the piece in the main picture.

* Note the pinkish off-white glaze, and the brownish body, which is exposed where the glaze has worn away on the rim. These features are typical of this early group of wares.

* Tugio was commissioned to make about 1,000 apothecary's vessels of various forms for the Ospedale – this slightly angular, egg-shaped jar is found in many international collections.

* Considered the beginnings of true maiolica, these "oak-leaf" jars today fetch five-figure sums under the hammer.

Palette

Early wares are primarily decorated in manganese-brown and copper-green, a combination used extensively around the Mediterranean world during the Middle Ages.

Around the beginning of the 15thC, cobalt blue was added to the palette, and was used either as a flat wash, or more thickly applied so that the colour stood out in slight relief, a technique also known as *impasto*. While early 15thC maiolica is still crude, designs and forms are beginning to become more complex.

The restricted palette of this Florentine or Faentine dish from the second half of the 15thC, is indicative of the period. The central flower head, painted in two tones of blue, is a feature of the Gothic style which followed on from the archaic period. On the broad border the design of serpentine motifs and radiating lines is known as San Bernadino rays, and was particularly popular on Faenza and Deruta maiolica.

This excavated double-handled Orvieto scudella made during in the early 15thC, and typically decorated in brown and green, is well potted but still relatively crude. The simple pattern is governed by the contours of the vessel (later in the 16thC the shape became secondary to the decoration).

* Hatching (a decorative technique which used a network of fine lines to create the effect of shading) as a ground is common on these early wares.

* Old maiolica is rarely even, close examination should reveal some warping or sagging.

This Faenza albarello, or dry drug jar c.1480, illustrates how the dull early 15thC colours were later balanced by the addition of ochre and a pale, turquoise green. Peacock feather motifs were particularly favoured by the potters of Faenza and Deruta. The central band of spiky flowerheads and scrolling tendrils was also used extensively as a filler pattern on late Gothic or "Severe" style maiolica, revealing the clay which will have absorbed a lot of dirt over the years making it appear much darker than it is. A fresh break will generally show a pale, buff-coloured body.

71

FLORENCE
& FAENZA

Faenza quartieri bowl with slight damage to the rim, c.1530-40; dia. 16in (40.6cm); value code C/D

Identification checklist for early 16thC Faentine
quartieri wares
1. Does the palette feature ochre or sienna and
an intense, dark, purplish blue?
2. Is the rim wide and decorated?
3. Is the decoration on the rim divided into six
or eight panels?
4. Does the design feature bold, scrolling foliage?
5. Is the piece in reasonable condition?

Florence
Important principally during the
15thC when maiolica was in its
infancy, the output of the Florentine potteries mainly comprised
pharmaceutical wares; flatware
appear to have been less common.
Using a reddish clay, objects were
painted in the sombre colours of
this period; initially manganese,
green and blue; later ochre was
added to the palette. After c.1550,
allegorical figure subjects based
on printed material first appear,
an early version of the *istoriato*
style that was developed in
areas such as Urbino.

Caffaggiolo
Situated near Florence, and
active some time later, potters
in Caffaggiolo produced some
of the most beautiful Italian
maiolica c.1500-30 in a factory
that, for a time, was under the
patronage of the Medici family
of Florence. Some pieces are
marked which has aided attribution of wares to Caffaggiolo.
  Caffaggiolo maiolica feature
a distinctive palette, including a
brownish or dark-cherry-red,
a thickly-applied, strong, dark
blue, orange, lemon-yellow, and
a clear transparent green.

* *Istoriato*: wares featuring narrative paintings, which form a small part of the output in the early 16thC.
* *Quartieri*: where the rim of a dish is divided into six, eight or more panels, as seen in the main picture.
* *Compendiario*: wares decorated in a restricted palette on a thick, white, Faenza glaze.
* *Berettino*: a pale blue wash covering the entire surface of a drug jar or dish. This method was also used on Venetian maiolica.

Painted with the arms of Pittigardi of Florence, this footed drug jar was made during the second half of the 15thC. The repeated stylized foliate background is based directly on Hispano-moresque ware produced near Valencia.
* Spanish lustre pottery was a strong influence on 15thC Italian maiolica.

Faenza
Still in production today, potteries in Faenza have been predominant since the second half of the 15thC. The dish in the main picture, decorated with bold scrolling foliage in the *quartieri* style, is painted in a characteristic palette, including ochre or sienna, and a dark, purplish blue.

The cool colours and the stiff postures of the figures on this dish c.1525, characterize the early *istoriato* style. The frieze-like composition and the blue-dominated palette, shown here, give an ethereal quality to Faenza wares of the early 16thC.

* The decoration on the base of the piece in the main picture is also typical; the splayed foot allows the piece to be hung up for decorative purposes.

Decorative styles
The following styles of decoration are characteristic of Faenza wares.
* Bold swirling Gothic foliage, bryony flowers and peacock feather motifs in the latter 15thC.

This vase and cover, dated 1558, is a rare and early example of the *compendiario* style, where the palette is reduced to blue, and detailed in yellow and ochre. The decoration on this piece is unusually dense.

DERUTA

One of a pair of Deruta wet-drug jars, dated 1507
ht 11in (27.9cm); value code A

Identification checklist for 16thC Deruta wares
1. Is the piece heavily potted?
2. Is the design and execution relatively simple or primitive?
3. Is the subject matter a portrait in profile or a religious subject?
4. If there is a border, does it feature a repeated geometric pattern or stylized vegetation?
5. If a large dish, is the underside washed in a greenish lead glaze?
6. If lustred, is the design highlighted in a greyish cobalt blue?
7. If painted in non-lustre colours, are the dominant colours ochre and greyish blue?

Deruta
Situated in Umbria in central Italy, perhaps somewhat detached from the mainstream of Faenza and Urbino, Deruta and potteries in the surrounding area produced bold, slightly primitive wares with a few brilliant exceptions. Decoration usually featured simple, repeated motifs, but occasionally piece are found with figure subjects.

The figures used within the designs were often derived from local artists such as Pietro Perugino (c.1445-1523) and his pupil Pintoricchio (c.1454-1513), and favoured religious person-ages, especially St. Francis, a local saint.

Output

Most Deruta wares were everyday items made for local consumption, such as plates, vases and albarelli. Plaques for religious purposes were also produced.
* About one tenth of the output was lustre wares (see below).

Compared with maiolica of the previous century, the drug jar in the main picture underlines the advances made during the High Renaissance (c.1490-1520). The sweeping contours demonstrate the mastery of the potter. The ambitious subject matter of the decoration, which includes muscular figures surrounded by grotesquerie, shows the imaginative use of current influences. Warm, earthy tones contrast with the more sepulchral shades found on earlier Archaic and Gothic styles.

This polychrome albarello c.1530, is an example of a typical Deruta form, with sharply angled shoulders, which are slightly wider than the flared base.
* It is decorated in the bold large-scale manner and colouring that is characteristic of Deruta, but which is also very similar to the wares of Castelli at this date (the Castelli albarello would probably be more cylindrical).
* Surrounding the portrait is dense, wave-like vegetation which distinguishes this type from the more controlled and smaller-scale patterns of Faenza or Urbino.

Lustre wares

Deruta was one of the few centres in Italy which produced lustre ware. Possibly because of the relative isolation of the area from the other main maiolica producing regions, the wares of Deruta are relatively simple to categorize.
* The potteries specialized in lustre ware from about 1500 until just after 1550.

A feature of the lustre output was the use of cobalt blue to highlight the gold lustre design, seen here on this double-handled jar, c.1530. In the centre there is a half-length portrait of a *bella donna* or beautiful woman, a favoured subject on Deruta (although it was also used in a more ambitious manner in Urbino). Surrounding the main theme are bands of simple, repeated, semi-geometric motifs, and bold scrolling foliage which resembles wrought iron work.

Based on a metal original, a surprising number of dishes designed to hold ewers (*bacile da versatore*), such as this one c.1530-40, have survived. The type of decoration seen here is arguably the most common in Italian maiolica: a formal arrangement of alternate geometric and foliate patterns. While the front of the dish is decorated in the standard scheme of blue and yellow lustre on a warm pinkish white tin-glaze, the reverse is simply washed in an olive or brownish lead-glaze.

URBINO &
RELATED WARES

An Urbino istoriato dish depicting the Rape of Proserpine, c.1530
dia. 12in (30.5cm); value code A

Identification checklist for Urbino and related wares
1. Is the piece relatively thinly potted?
2. Is the glaze a warm, off-white tone?
3. Are there irregular areas of bluish or greenish tones in the glaze on the underside?
4. Is the decoration narrative?
5. Is the painting finely executed, but not stiff and mechanical?
6. Do the colours include copper green, yellow, ochre, olive brown, black (actually an extremely dark brown), and a bright cobalt blue?
7. Is the rim painted in yellow ochre?

Istoriato wares
Urbino and the nearby towns of Castel Durante and Gubbio were the home of *istoriato* maiolica, where the entire surface of a piece was painted with a religious or mythological subject. From about 1520 onwards, the potters in this region made considerable quantities of narrative wares, often based on a collection of stories by the Roman writer, Ovid (43 BC-18 AD), called the Metamorphoses. Ovid's work was extremely popular with writers and painters alike during the Renaissance. The leading exponents of *istoriato* included Nicola da Urbino, his son Francesco Durantino, and a close follower, Francesco Xanto Avelli da Rovigo.

The dish in the main picture is a good example of the *istoriato* tradition. By the 16thC the decoration had become more important than the shape of the piece, and the dish has simply been used as a canvas. This piece was painted by Nicola Gabriele Sbraghe, who often signed his work "Nicola da Urbino", who was perhaps the greatest exponent of *istoriato*.

* The palette of brown, green, ochre and blue was joined in the 16thC by a rich, amber-yellow, giving a brighter feel than Faentine *istoriato* wares.
* Also note the human forms, which are more animated, and the greater fluidity of the painting as a whole.

Another Urbino piece, this dish (above) c.1530, features Europa and the Bull, a favourite theme for *istoriato* painters, although they usually appear accompanied by other figures.
* The rim is heightened in yellow ochre, a common colour on *istoriato* from Urbino and other pottery towns along the north-eastern coast of Italy, such as Venice, Pesaro and Rimini.

Castel Durante

South west of Urbino, Castel Durante was the home of many great *istoriato* painters during the

16thC. The maiolica made there in the first 30 years of the 16thC, probably under the patronage of the Dukes of Urbino, is some of the most beautiful and influential pottery ever made.

The flat dish or *tagliere*, below left, dated 1539 forms part of a confinement set that was used to serve food to women during the final stages of pregnancy. It is appropriately painted with a mother holding her infant.
* The rim is decorated with trophies on a blue ground, a popular theme on Castel Durante and Urbino wares from about 1530 onwards.

Gubbio

Gubbio maiolica was renowned for its gold and ruby-lustre decoration, especially c.1500-50, where the technique was practised successfully by Maestro Giorgio Andreoli.

Andreoli and his sons highlighted conventional polychrome wares, either from their own workshop or sent from Urbino, in red and gold lustre. This example, dated 1524, bears the arms of Vigieri of Savona within a wide border. The only colours used underneath the lustre were cobalt blue and green; the remainder is either gold or ruby lustre.
* It is usual for Andreoli to inscribe the reverse with his monogram and the date as he has done on this dish.

Later 16thC decoration

In the latter half of the 16thC the grotesque (see glossary) played an increasing role in decoration. First confined to borders, as seen in the lustre ware dish above, it was eventually incorporated into the main or central theme, thereby reducing it in importance.

SICILY, CASTELLI & SIENA

A small Sicilian albarello, probably Caltagirone, 17thC; ht 8in (20.3cm); value code F/G

* An identification checklist for this group of wares would be inappropriate because of the variety of forms and styles discussed here.

Sicily
In Sicily there were about half-a-dozen manufacturing centres, including Palermo which was by far the best. Most Sicilian pottery is of a derivative nature, based on Faenza, Venice and other mainland wares.

Caltagirone
The Sicilian town of Caltagirone was probably one of the most productive centres in Sicily. Note the somewhat clumsy, old-fashioned scrollwork painted in a typical pale greyish cobalt, which can be seen on the albarello in the main picture.

Sicilian albarelli were often tall and sharply waisted, differing from the squatter versions produced in central and northern Italy at this time.
    Features of Caltagirone pottery are as follows:
* a base that is often smeared with a thin wash of greyish, milky glaze
* the use of manganese as an outline, and a strong use of blue and ochre.

Palermo
Potters in Palermo (the capital of Sicily) produced some of the most refined Sicilian maiolica,

such as this albarello made c.1600. Portraits of saints were very popular here and in Venice, and there is often confusion between the two. As a rule, Venetian brushwork has a more painterly feel than the rather stiffer handling evident here.
* The rope-twist pattern and the feathery scrolls within the borders seen here, are found on 16thC Faentine maiolica.

Castelli
Situated in the centre of Italy, near the east coast, the town of Castelli is celebrated for its narrative wares, based on engravings by a number of artists.

Plaques were produced in some quantity in and around Castelli throughout the 18thC. Earlier examples exist, but these usually feature religious subjects. The scenes were very picturesque, such as the one above, painted by Dr. Francesco Grue, and dated 1727, featuring an Arcadian landscape and classical ruins.
* Other Castelli wares include albarelli, double-handled bottles and dragon-spouted syrup pots.

Other Sicilian centres
Potters in Trapani made coarser, more clumsily-decorated pieces than those in Palermo.

This albarello from the early 17thC has less crisply-defined contours than the piece from Palermo, see above left, and is taller and looks unstable.
* Other features usually found on Trapani are the dark purplish cobalt blue, and the use of small diagonal dashes around the neck.
* The wreath surrounding the blue and white strapwork frame was a feature used extensively on Deruta wares.

Siena
* Active from at least the 13thC, Siena is chiefly notable the fine, intricate work produced from about 1500 onwards.
* Decoration usually comprises small geometric or repeating patterns built up around the piece.
* Saints or other religious subjects enclosed within a tight scrolling border of foliage or arabesques are found. Known as *alla porcellana*, this style was supposedly derived from Chinese porcelain, but is more likely to be based on Turkish or other Islamic pottery, which was itself influenced by Chinese Ming porcelain.
* Later Siena maiolica is noted for its wares with narrative scenes, similar in tone to contemporary Castelli.

Collecting
* Of all Italian maiolica, drug jars are the most widely collected items. Relatively common pieces with some damage, can be bought for reasonably modest prices (these wares are rarely found in perfect condition, so expect chips on the rim or cracks in the body).
* Hollow wares from the 17th and 18thC in relatively good condition, can be bought for even less.

FRENCH POTTERY

One of a pair of faience lions, Rouen, 18thC

Only in the 16thC did French potteries begin to produce high-quality pottery. These early wares include lead-glazed items by Bernard Palissy (Bernard de Tuileries), made at Saintes (1542-62) and subsequently in Paris. His pottery is characterized by figures and decoration comprising relief ornamentation covered with coloured glazes, mainly yellow, blue and grey, with brown and manganese. His best-known pieces are dishes and plates modelled with leaves, snakes, lizards, insects, shells and other natural objects in high relief. These items inspired many copies during the 19thC in France, Germany, England and Portugal, but these are generally crude in comparison.

There was also a group known as Henri Deux wares, which comprised a range of similar types of wares made during the reign of François I (1515-47) and Henri II (1547-59). This group included *faience à neillure*, a fine-glazed earthenware with impressed decoration filled with clays of contrasting colour, originally made at Saint Porchaire in south west France. Similar wares were also said to be made at nearby Oiron, and are known as *faience d'Oiron*.

Italian potters settling in France had provided the main impetus for the development of pottery in different parts of the country. There were three main centres. In the south around Lyon and Montpellier, Italian craftsmen recorded in c.1510 began to produce Italian-style tin-glazed wares, and it is this date which is usually accepted as the starting point for the production of fine tin-glazed ware in France. In Rouen, between 1530 and 1564, Masseot Abaquesne produced painted tile decorations (mainly commissioned for churches and large houses), and also Italian-style, wet and dry drug jugs, distinguished from High Renaissance wares by their angularity.

The development of pottery production around Nevers, located on the Loire in Nivernais, central France, was very important. A family of Italian potters settled here in the

16thC, encouraged by Lodovico Gonzaga, a soldier of fortune who had acquired the Duchy of Nevers. This city was to become the most prominent manufacturing centre in the 17thC. Spanish potters were also an important influence in France during the 16thC, as they carried out commissions for tilework throughout the country.

During the 17thC, there was a move away from the production of Italianate wares: local styles started to develop, and new influences became more important, especially imports of Chinese porcelain in the second quarter of the 17thC, and French baroque designs. Nevers pottery was particularly influenced by late Ming and Chinese export wares; situated near to the Court in Paris, they were particularly aware of the fashions of the day.

By the end of the 17thC, Rouen had become the main centre. This was due to its location on the banks of the Seine, its proximity to Paris, access to good local clays, and the large-scale melting down of silver ordered by Louis XIV in 1709, in order to pay for the cost of the war of the Spanish succession. Following this last development, pottery was used to replace the lost silver wares. Late baroque styles, such as *lambrequin* (a scalloped border comprising drapery, lacework, leaves and scrollwork) became more rational and geometric. A particularly notable decorative form was *style rayonnant* with concentric designs in blue, white, and sometimes red and black. Potters in Rouen were also influenced by Chinese *famille verte* porcelain, with its palette of transparent green, iron-red, blue, yellow and purple. These pieces were highly regarded, and many were in turn copied and exported by Chinese porcelain manufacturers.

At this time factories in southern France, around Moustiers and Marseilles, began to produce distinctive types of faïence using *grand-feu*, high-fired colours. Moustiers wares made c.1710-40 are decorated with elaborate designs by Jean Bérain, that feature mythological grotesque figures and half-figures, vases of flowers, drapes, balustrades and urns. Joseph Olerys was an important figure throughout this area during the first half of the 18thC. His pottery produced polychrome wares with elaborate borders comprising flowers and medallions with mystical subjects. Olerys' wares were the inspiration for many potteries in the area, and there is, therefore, a variation in quality of apparently similar pieces made at this time.

In the mid-18thC low-fired, *petit-feu* enamels, a technique copied from German porcelain, were adopted by some French faïenciers. They followed the French rococo style, with fluid, shell-like forms and elaborate surfaces, white bodies and thick glazes. Wares made in Strasbourg represent the extreme of rococo decoration, whereas those produced around Paris are more restrained. During the second half of the 18thC the manufacture of *faience* went into decline owing to competition from French porcelain and from English creamware. Production did continue into the 19thC, but in a greatly reduced form.

FRENCH CENTRES

The earliest distinctive French pottery is probably earthenware made in the 14thC, made from unglazed buff material decorated in red. Slightly later, unglazed, grey wares were found. Made during the 14th or 15thC are a group of yellow-glazed jugs and mugs, and also some brownwares with applied decoration. In the late 15th and early 16thC, relief-moulded dishes with *sgraffiato* decoration have been found. These pieces are associated with Beauvais, to the north of Paris.

These early lead-glazed wares were the forerunners of 16thC pottery produced at La Chapelle-des-pots, Avignon and Beauvais, and inspired the development of the more refined 16thC pieces by Bernard Palissy in Saintes and subsequently Paris. His distinctive wares are modelled with relief decoration comprising fish, reptiles, insects, snakes and other natural objects. Coloured with blue, green, maganese and ochre, they are covered in a shiny lead glaze. Other famous groups of 16thC wares are the *faiences Henri Deux*, and *faience à neillure* made in Saint Porchaire, and *faience d'Orion* made at nearby Oiron. These wares did not have an influence on later French pottery.

Italian potters provided much of the influence over pottery throughout France during the 16thC. Maiolica was produced in Brou, Rouen, Nîmes, Lyon and Nevers, which is amost indistinguishable from Italian wares.

The most important early factory was at Nevers. The first recorded potters in Nevers were two Italians who were granted a *privilège*, purchased from the king, which allowed them to make pottery in the town for the next 30 years. They produced *istoriato* wares, and pieces with *compendiario* and *berretino* decoration (see pp.72-3). Some of the most famous wares produced at Nevers featured a rich, blue ground, with formal patterns in ochre and white. Nevers remained important throughout the 17thC. The Chinese influence which was adopted by most European potters at this time, is seen in abstract, Oriental-style themes, rather than the superficial imitation carried out by potters in the Netherlands.

Gradually a native French style developed. One of the earliest was at Rouen, where fine, tin-glazed wares were produced by Masseot Abasquesne, between 1530 and his death in 1564. The principal output of his factory consisted of decorative tile panels designed and made for noblemen and for the Church, and large sets of apothecaries' jars with distinctive forms.

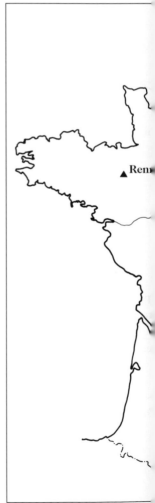

▲ Ren

FRENCH POTTERY

Rouen had become the most important centre by the end of the 17thC, producing faience which influenced potters in Paris, St. Cloud, Lille, Saint-Amand-les-Eaux, Marseilles and Strasbourg, and later, rich, polychrome wares in Chinese and rococo styles. Moustiers became important in the late 17thC, making pictorial panels in styles that were widely imitated. In the 18thC, enamel-painted wares in the style of contemporary porcelain were first produced at the factory of Paul Hannong in Strasbourg. This style was quickly taken up at Niderviller, Marseilles, Rouen and Moustiers.

In the late 18th and early 19thC, potteries began to imitate the cream-coloured earthenware made at Staffordshire in England, that was called *faience fine* in France. This was made at Lunéville, Bellvue, Saint Clément, Paris and Orléans. Other Staffordshire-influenced wares made in France included stonewares and marbled pottery.

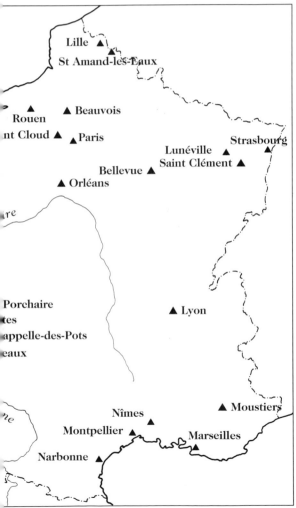

16TH & 17THC POTTERY

A Manerbé or Pré d'Auge oval dish, School of Palissy, 17thC; lgth. 19in (48cm); value code F

Identification checklist for 16th and 17thC Palissy-type wares
1. Has the piece been moulded in relief with subjects such as plants, shells, fish, snakes, insects and reptiles?
2. Is the moulding very realistic?
3. Does the design feature water or a stream?
4. Is the glaze thick?
5. Are the colours dark and shiny?
6. Do they include brown, manganese, ochre, green and blue?
7. Is the surface textured?

Bernard Palissy (c.1510-90)
A French Renaissance potter, Bernard Palissy, made multi-coloured lead-glazed earthenwares at Saintes, France, 1542-62, and thereafter near Paris, at the Palais de Tuileries. They are moulded in high relief with reptiles, shells, fish, plants and animals, usually on a ground that features water or a stream. Blue, green, brown and yellow are the predominant colours. Dishes and plates are the most commonly-found wares, although some vases, basins and ewers were also made.
* Original Palissy wares are rare – none of his actual work is known to have been marked – but those made by his followers, such as the piece in the main picture, are also high quality and relatively inexpensive.

Also from the School of Palissy, the decoration on this dish is painted in characteristic dark, shiny lead glaze.
* Most 16th and 17thC Palissy or Palissy-type wares will be damaged in some way. Pieces with a few chips and cracks are usually less expensive, and can be a good way to begin a collection.
* Palissy wares are copied by a Portuguese pottery at Caldhas da Rainha; these are usually marked.

French tin-glazed ware

The tradition of manufacturing tin-glazed earthenware, termed "faience" in France, was established mainly by immigrant Italian potters at the beginning of the 16thC, although there are earlier (late 14thC) records of Spanish and Italian craftsmen working in a number of areas of France. These potters worked in the current Mediterranean style using manganese-brown as an outline and copper-green as a wash.

Lyon

Italian potters had settled in Lyon by at least 1512, and this date is generally accepted as the starting point for fine tin-glazed ware. Pieces from Lyon are difficult to distinguish from Urbino or other Italian maiolica, or indeed from the early products of Nevers.

* The existence of one dish in the British museum has made it possible to attribute a number of wares to Lyons. Painted with the biblical subject of Pharaoh's rod turning into a serpent, the piece is inscribed "Leons" (Lyon), and is dated 1582.

Nevers

The city of Nevers on the Loire in Nivernais in central France, became the most prominent manufacturing centre in the 17thC when French potters gradually broke away from the Italian styles.

* The Nevers baluster jar below, is a good example of a transitional style. The narrative subject (Perseus and Andromeda from Greek mythology), was popular on Italian maiolica from Urbino, but the free brushwork, the predominance of blue and ochre, and the thickly-drawn waves, are all typical of Nevers faience.

In the middle of the 17thC, a native style emerged, although the baroque designs borrowed heavily from Rome via the work of painters Nicolas Poussin and Simon Vouet, who studied there, and whose images were often the source for the pottery artists at Nevers.

In the third quarter of the 17thC century the use of figure or landscape subjects within a shaped cartouche on a lively scrolled ground became a common practice, especially on the borders of dishes, many of which were moulded. Figures drawn from pastoral romances, such as on this polychrome basin from c.1650-80, appeared regularly on Nevers faience.

Chinese influence

Imports of Chinese porcelain had a strong influence on French faience from about 1640 onwards; the form of the jar (below left) is essentially Chinese. It was an adaptation rather than a straightforward reproduction, sometimes blended with European decorative style and form.

Blue and white wares

French faience painted with blue and white Chinese-style designs are similar in many ways to Dutch Delft wares, but in general can be distinguished as follows:

* Dutch designs are usually crisper and more detailed, with almost spidery outlines.
* The manganese outlines used by Dutch potters appear dark chocolate brown, French outlines are softer and warmer.
* Manganese and cobalt glaze on French wares often appears mottled.
* On French pieces, line margins frequently melt during firing to give a wavy effect.

Marks

With few exceptions early wares are unmarked. The Lyon dish cited above and a handful of late 16thC Nevers or Nîmes pieces are dated or inscribed.

FAÏENCE I: ROUEN

A Rouen faïence helmet-shaped ewer, 1700-20; ht 11in (28cm); value code E

Identification checklist for 18thC Rouen faïence
1. Is the piece heavily potted?
2. If visible, is the clay red in colour?
3. Is the glaze relatively thick?
4. Does the glaze dribble slightly?
5. Does the decoration comprise stylized leaf or flower motifs?
6. Is the decoration dense?
7. Does the piece have a bluish glaze?
8. Where thin, is the glaze pinkish rather than bluish?

Rouen

For much of the 17thC, Nevers was the most important manufacturer of faïence, but in the last decade the city of Rouen assumed the leading role. Located down river from Paris, Rouen was ideally placed for the shipment of materials, fuel and of course its products. Little is known of pottery production in Rouen between the death of Masseot Abaquesne (c.1564) and 1644 when a privilege was granted for

the manufacture of tin-glazed ware. This privilege was acquired by Edme Poterat, whose family retained the monopoly until 1694 when a number of other potteries were then established.

The wars of Louis XIV provided an unexpected bonus for the potters of Rouen; in 1689 and again in 1709, in a state of national emergency and in a desperate need for campaign funds, the King and his courtiers had their silverware melted down.

Deprived of table ware and other domestic utensils, the nobility bought faience to replace their silver, some of which was decorated with their coats-of-arms.
* One of the more popular forms in Rouen faience, the helmet shape seen in the main picture, is also found in silver both in France and in England. Many of these were made by Protestant Huguenot silversmiths, forced into exile following the Revocation of the Edict of Nantes in 1685, which made Protestantism illegal. Here the traditional blue decoration has been enhanced by the addition of a strong red – an innovation from c.1700 – reflecting the fashionable Japanese Imari wares being imported at the time.
* Just visible on edge of the footrim where the bluish glaze stops, is the red clay of Rouen.

Decoration

At Rouen, in a break away from the early baroque style epitomized by Nevers, the potters decorated their wares in a completely different manner. Although this new style is similar in some respects to work by Renaissance engravers, it appears to derive from the sort of ornament found in bookbinding, wrought iron-work, and in particular, lace.

Based on contemporary baroque silver, this early 18thC sugar sifter is painted in cobalt blue with the intricate patterns characteristic of Rouen.

* The designs are composed of small formalized leaf or flower motifs which look like an old-fashioned ornamented napkin. Whatever the size of the object to be decorated, whether it was a massive meat-dish or a little cruet pot, the motifs were simply built up around it until the space was filled with the decoration.

By the second decade of the 18thC the popularity of polychrome wares had increased, and decorative styles had became loose, and less symmetrical, with Chinoiserie themes merging with the prevailing rococo style.

Material

* Late 17thC or early 18thC Rouen produced a heavily potted ware made of red clay, whereas clay used in Nevers during the same period was thinner and buff-coloured.
* Only subtle differences exist in glazes: Rouen wares tend to have a slightly more uneven surface, although this is not always true.

Painted in familiar *grand-feu* (high-fired) colours, this dish from c.1740, decorated with slightly stilted interpretation of Chinoiserie, belongs to a small group of wares which appear to have been inspired by embroidered designs. Other Oriental themes including pavillions, landscapes and scenes including figures, were also popular.
* The strange pyramidal structure to the left is a misunderstanding of a zig-zag fence in a Chinese garden.
* The cross-hatching on the border is also derived from Chinese export porcelain of the Kangxi (1662-1722) period.
* The shape of the dish above is once again based on contemporary silver wares, but the combination of straight lines and reversing curves, is also found on baroque mirrors, and in the style of pathways from monumental gardens in the early 18thC.

FAÏENCE II: OTHER CENTRES

A Strasbourg faïence oval dish, c.1750; ht 18in (46cm); value code E.

Identification checklist for mid-18thC Strasbourg faïence

1. Is the piece detailed and crisply moulded?
2. Does the glaze have a pinkish-white tone?
3. Has the piece been painted using pastel shades such as pink?
4. Is the brushwork meticulous?
5. Does the piece feature a floral or Chinoiserie design?
6. If floral, are the flowers realistic?
7. Does the piece have a coloured border (puce was often used)?

Other centres

By c.1725 other centres producing faïence had developed in the south and east of France. During the next 50 years the great factories of Moustiers, Marseilles, and above all Strasbourg, flourished, with some of the most beautiful tin-glazed wares ever made.

After 1750, many factories experienced competition from more refined porcelain, and also from less expensive wares. These problems were exacerbated by the economic instability of revolutionary France.

Moustiers

One of the most important faïence centres from c.1679, wares made by factories in Moustiers were widely imitated in the South of France, Spain and Italy. The faïence of the town rose to artistic importance under Pierre Clérissy, a member of a family of potters.

A more "modelled" version of decorative style popularized in Rouen (see pp. 86-7), that continued well into the 1730s, are the late "grotesque" ornaments based on the engravings of Jean Bérain (1638-1711) and others. Especially popular at Moustiers, this style of decoration comprised an intricate scroll framework arranged symmetrically with tiers of figures or "terms", similar to supporting pillars or pedestals found in furniture and architecture.

This small Moustiers tureen and cover, c.1750-60, is an example of a popular style from the Laugier-Olerys factory (est.1738), and is painted in a typical Moustiers colour scheme with a prominent ochre combined with green and blue (although absent from this piece manganese-brown or purple is also used).
* Garlands that are suspended from extremely thin threads, are a feature of this factory; occasionally they support figure medallions, in a style known as *à guirlandes et medaillons* decoration.
* Although this particular piece is unmarked, similar pieces sometimes carry the letters "OL", the initials of the proprietors, Joseph Olerys and his brother-in-law Jean-Baptiste Laugier.

Strasbourg

Factories in Strasbourg in the 18thC produced some of the finest French faience and set a fashion for meticulous enamel painting that was copied elsewhere in France, including Moustiers, Bordeaux, Rouen and Marseilles.

Fleurs fine or *fleurs de Strasbourg* were painted in *petit-feu* enamels (see below), the detailed brushwork is typical of the early phase of this style of flower painting, using either German or Swiss engravings as a source. The quality of the painting improved over the next ten years.
* The dish in the main picture, c.1750, based on an original silver piece, and therefore crisply moulded, is from a service made for the Elector Clemens August of Cologne, by the Strasbourg factory (est.1721) during its finest period, when it was run by Joseph Hannong (1669-1739) and his family.
* Note the warm pinkish white tones of the glaze which is typical of Strasbourg.
* The rim is highlighted in puce, a colour favoured for border embellishment by faïenciers and French porcelain manufacturers,

as a substitute for gold – gilding was banned by royal edict to hinder competition with Louis XV's own factory at Vincennes-Sèvres.

Petit-feu enamelling

A major change took place around 1750 with the introduction of *petit-feu* enamels. As the name implies this palette was fired in a low temperature muffle kiln, a technique first used on ceramics in Germany in the 17thC. The method allowed a very wide range of colours with subtle pastel variations, including pink or puce.

While remaining loyal to the use of Chinoiserie, factories which perfected *petit-feu* enamelling during the 18thC began to paint in a more delicate way:
* *Strasbourg*: celebrated botanical studies after woodblock prints.
* *Marseilles* (see below): more naturalistic flowers, quay scenes and even the "bouillabaisse" style of various fish and shell fish.
* *Moustiers*: curious clumps of *solanum* (potato flower), short, misshapen figures and fantastic creatures, and oval panels of classical figures hung with thread-stemmed festoons.

Marseilles

Potters in Marseilles in the second half of the 18thC also worked using *petit-feu* enamels.

Painted with a looser and more spontaneous design than those on wares produced in northern France, this sparingly-decorated plate features a Chinoiserie design. Made at the Veuve Perrin factory (1748-1793) c.1760, this is a typical example of Marseilles faience.
* Similar wares were produced at the other eleven Marseilles factories.
* This piece bears the VP factory monogram.

FAIENCE WARES

Dining table wares

The French have made an art of the dinner table, not simply their cuisine, but also their overall presentation. It is probably true to say that dining wares, apart from basic flatware, are more varied and ambitious in France than anywhere else. The melting-down of silver wares during the reign of Louis XIV (1643-1715), to finance his military campaigns, led to the production of a wide range of domestic pottery based on silver forms. These included:

* spice-boxes
* sugar casters
* helmet-shaped ewers
* snuff boxes
* inkstands
* candlesticks

The crucifix (above), was made at the Leroy factory in Marseilles (1749-c.1793). Established by Louis Leroy who died in 1788, the business was then run for a short time by his son Antoine (d.1790).

Figures

Faience figures were not widely made, indeed some factories produced no figures at all. This is because it is extremely difficult to model figures in low fired "short" clay with the movement or definition expected of porcelain modellers. A further disadvantage is that the thickish, tin glaze obscures and softens the contours of the figure.

Regional centres of faience manufacture such as Lille, Nevers and Bordeaux produced simply-modelled, devotional figures of saints, often with particular local importance. In general, these are

* tureens, such as this one made in Strasbourg c.1765. The painting on this piece differs from the natural fleurs de Strasbourg (see pp.88-9); the stylized design is based on contemporary Chinese exportware. Another important difference is the black outlining of the flowers.
* other decorative objects for use as table centrepieces.

Some factories made religious items such as holy-water stoops (*benitiers*) and devotional figures.

decorated in the *grand-feu* colours of manganese, yellow-ochre, blue and green, sometimes with the name inscribed on the base. More advanced rococo and Neo-classical figures and groups were made at Paul Hannong's Strasbourg factory, and also at Marseilles and Niderviller. These are ambitiously modelled, often in elegant forms. Usually painted with *petit-feu* enamel colours, the palette is dominated by puce, yellow and blue; the results are frequently close to soft-paste porcelain.

* Subjects are usually contemporary: shepherds, musicians, lovers and animals.

Other decorative wares

The more sophisticated factories such as Strasbourg, Sceaux, Niderviller and Marseilles made some large-scale decorative pieces, including wall-cisterns and basins, *jardinières*, bulb pots for growing flowers, and *bouquetières* for displaying cut flowers. (*Bouquetières* are cut with holes where flower stems are inserted.)

* A number of extremely complex clocks were also produced.
* The factories at Rouen made game boards and classical portrait busts.
* Good examples of high quality French faience, the pieces in the picture above left are (from left to right), a Rouen faience sauce boat c.1730, a faience shaped dish, probably Marseilles c.1750 and a Rouen pewter-mounted hot water jug, c.1770. All feature skillful painting, strong colours and crisp moulding.

Marks

* The use of marks on French faience was almost an entirely random activity: while some of the very finest pieces carry no mark at all, very many third-rate pieces are marked.
* Most marks are painted in puce, blue or black. Some are initials or a representative picture (rebus) based on the name of the proprietor, such as the combined "I" and "H" which stands for Joseph Hannong of Strasbourg, or the anchor used on pieces from the faience factory at Sceaux near Paris, which is derived from the coat of arms of the Duke of Penthièvre (Grand Admiral of France).
* As well as the factory mark, there may also be painter's marks, and model or size numbers. The wares of Joseph Hannong are often numbered.

Collecting

French faience frequently appears at auction. While large, rare pieces are expensive, smaller items, such as simple dishes or sauce boats, from Strasbourg and Marseilles are more accessibly priced.

Tea wares

A wide range of faience tea wares were also made in France during the 18thC. Made in Moustiers, the items (below) have been made with an unsual ground colour, but they feature the high quality painting that is typical of this region. The naturalistic flowers seen here were a popular motif. Other subjects included figures, and mythological and pastoral themes.

* The enamels on later Moustiers wares are smooth and glossy.
* Pieces from Moustiers are less common than those from other centres.

NORTHERN EUROPEAN POTTERY

A Kiel faience tray painted by Abraham Liehamer, dated 1769

There are two primary groups in northern European pottery; first the relatively humble wares made for local consumption and more refined items with a wider appeal and directed at a wider market. The first type includes Habener wares of Austria and Hungary. These are rarely found in any quantities outside their own countries, and therefore appear infrequently in the auction rooms of foreign countries. The second category includes tin-glazed earthenware which because of its porcellaneous appearance was intended for the comfortable classes in society who aspired to the porcelains used in grander household in say the 18thC.

Much of this section is devoted to tin-glazed earthenwares made in the north from the late 15th or early 16thC onwards. Beginning in Antwerp in around 1500 potters again pushed on to other locations in the Netherlands, setting up factories along the coast at Rotterdam, Haarlem and Amsterdam. They are also recorded as having moved from the Netherlands to Spain and in the 1560s to England where they founded potteries in Norwich and in London.

Until well into the 17thC, tin-glazed earthenwares followed the traditional Italian style but as time progressed diluted with local influences such as that of the mannerist designs of the Fontainebleau school on Netherlandish and even English pottery. However, by the 17thC, the importation of Chinese blue and white porcelain changed the picture entirely. The polychrome palette was mostly abandoned in favour of blue and white painted in the manner of late Ming *kraakporselein* or later the "Transitional" style which dominated the finer wares produced at Jingdezhen, the home of Chinese blue and white.

The rise of the town of Delft as the major tin-glazed pottery centre in the middle of the 17thC was a remarkable phenomenon. A large number of propitious factors ensuring its success (see pp.98-9). Over 30 potteries were active in Delft, and the wares produced were sold throughout northern Europe.

In the latter half of the 17thC, potters from Holland, presumably to find new and less competitive markets, established factories in Germany at Frankfurt, Hanau and Berlin. The earliest products from these factories are virtually indistinguishable from Dutch wares. While some early 18thC wares are similar to Delft ware, German potters evolved their own forms and decorative styles.

As well as "high-fired", colours German decorators also employed the low-fired enamels on their better wares from about 1680 on. While the major proportion of German potteries located in the southern half of the country, a few factories were established in Schleswig-Holstein, where they produced some of the best large-scale enamelled wares – for example, table tops, trays and centrepieces. During the 18thC, Schleswig-Holstein was part of the kingdom of Denmark and its wares, in common with the Scandinavian countries Norway and Sweden, Denmark itself made kindred wares inspired equally by Delft and Strasbourg pieces.

In Belgium, the Brussels factories were noted for their *tromp l'oeil* wares such as cabbage-leaf tureens, models of animals and birds based on Strasbourg wares, they were not as technically advanced as the French factory with inferior potting and a tendency to overfire the colours. While the Tournai factory did make faience in the first half of the 18thC few, if any, pieces can be attributed to it.

In the second category are the Rhenish stonewares, first produced in the early Middle Ages. By the 17thC these robust pieces were exported to France, England and Holland. Included here are the white-bodied and highly refined Siegburg *schnelle*, *schnabelkanne* and other forms applied with crisply moulded figure subjects or armorial devices. At the other end of the scale are the more cumbersome, fat-bellied bellarmines of Cologne and Frechen covered in a mottled brown "tigerskin" glaze. The wares of Raeren, while similar to Cologne before about 1560, represent some of the most intricate and complicated of all German stonewares. The best period is from c.1575-1600 when composite shaped jugs with a cylindrical frieze were applied with relief moulded figures. Covered in a deep, lustrous, brown salt-glaze they are generally smoother than their Cologne or Frechen counterparts.

Another important group is from Westerwald, a greybodied stoneware, mostly decorated in cobalt-blue and manganese with bold scrolling foliage or repeated stamped motifs, and sometimes applied with royal monograms, often of contemporary English monarchs.

Finally, the relatively scarce enamelled stonewares of Kreussen and Annaberg: they are painted in strong colours, in the manner of glass enamelling, with hunting scenes, pastoral landscapes or scrolling foliage, production of this type apparently ceasing in the 1730s.

NORTHERN EUROPEAN CENTRES

The main pottery-producing centres in northern Europe were based in present-day Holland and Germany. There is a large, complex network of centres situated in Germany, and as a result these are illustrated here.

One of the earliest German pottery-producing areas is around Cologne (Köln) in the Rhineland. Some of the most famous German pottery, high quality salt-glazed stoneware,

was produced in the Rhineland during the 16thC, in Cologne, Siegburg, Raeren and Westerwald. Several places in Saxony were important in the 17thC, such as Freiburg and Altenburg. Potters at Kreussen in Bavaria made a notable group of painted stonewares.

German faience was first produced in Hanau and Frankfurt-am-Maine, and pottery from these areas was for a long time

confused with wares from Delft in Holland. While the production of much German faience was dominated by imitations of blue and white Chinese porcelain, characteristic wares were also made. From c.1715-40 at Nuremburg and Bayreuth, a highly-individual, Baroque style was developed, with painting executed in bright, high-fired colours. In the mid-18thC the influence of porcelain (particularly wares from Meissen) is first seen, and faience painted with *petit-feu* enamel colours was made in Fulda, Höchst and Kunnersberg. The wares of Strasbourg (see pp.88-9) were also highly influential.

The main centres in Holland are fewer and better known than those located in Germany. They include Antwerp, Rotterdam, Amsterdam, Middleburg, Makkum, and most notably Delft. Tin-glazed wares were first made in Antwerp by Italian potters in the 16thC. The industry then began to move north, and production peaked with 17th and 18thC Delft wares. Dutch blue and white wares were a major influence in Europe.

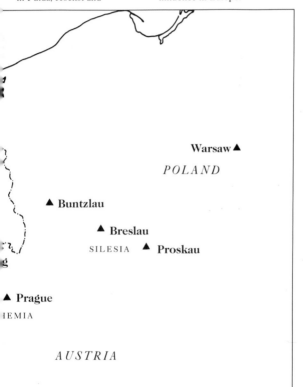

Warsaw ▲

POLAND

▲ **Buntzlau**

▲ **Breslau**

SILESIA ▲ **Proskau**

▲ **Prague**

IEMIA

AUSTRIA

Six polychrome glazed tiles, early 17thC;
5¼ x 5¼in (13 x 13cm); value code F

Identification checklist for early 17thC Dutch glazed tiles

1. Is the tile polychrome?
2. Do blue and ochre dominate the palette?
3. Does the decoration include flowers, birds or animals, portraits, ships and shipbuilding, soldiers or mythological figures?
4. Is the tile a standard size, 5¼ x 5¼in (13 x 13cm)?

Netherlands tin-glazed pottery

The first tin-glazed pottery was probably manufactured in the Netherlands at the beginning of the 16thC. Records indicate that Guido Andries (d. before 1541), an Italian immigrant possibly from Castel Durante, was making tiles and small useful wares in Antwerp by at least 1508. He and his family were leading figures in the spread of the maiolica tradition in northern Europe.

Netherlands maiolica

16th and early 17thC Dutch pottery inspired by Faentine and other northern Italian wares, is known as "Netherlands maiolica". In the late 16thC, many potters left Antwerp and established themselves in centres such as Rotterdam, Haarlem, Amsterdam and Dordrecht.

Tiles

The production of Dutch glazed tiles, such as the examples in the main picture, was very successful. First manufactured in Antwerp, together with wall panels and house signs, producers later moved further north, where the industry flourished.

* Makkum in Friesland, Middleburg, Gouda, Delft and Rotterdam were important centres of production.

Many different tile designs were produced, which included flowers, birds and animals (such as dogs, goats and seals).
* More unusual pieces feature portraits, ships and shipbuilding, soldiers and mythological figures, seen on the tiles in the main picture, and on the example above from Rotterdam, made during the first half of the 17thC.
* In the late 17thC polychrome tiles began to be replaced by blue or manganese monochrome designs, probably under the influence of Chinese porcelain (see below).

Decoration
By the middle of the 16thC the decoration on Dutch pottery began to show the influence of the local northern designers, Vredeman de Vries of Leeuwarden, and Cornelis Bos and Frans Floris of Antwerp. Italian-style designs were replaced with bold strapwork cartouches, scrolled devices imitating ironwork and fantastical figures. The most common colours are:
* copper-green
* cobalt-blue
* ochre
* yellow.
(Manganese-brown does not appear to have been used on early Netherlands wares.)

Decorative influences
During the early years of the 17thC, the industry encountered a new source of inspiration that heralded the rise of Dutch pottery in Europe. Imports of late Chinese Ming wares, known as *kraakporselein* after the large ships or *kraak* that brought the items to Holland from the Far East, encouraged Dutch potteries to discard the bright maiolica colour scheme and replace it with a blue and white palette.

This blue and white dish from the second half of the 17thC is painted in Chinese export style; a large number of similar pieces were produced, and even today can be acquired for very modest sums.

As in so many European pottery centres in the 17thC there is often a fusion of Italian and Chinese designs. The tin-glazed wares made in Rotterdam are a good example of this idiosyncratic style, and this dish from the early 17thC features a typical Western religious image, the Madonna and Child, together with a Chinese-style, panelled border.
    Faience was first made in Rotterdam in c.1612. The importance of the town as a pottery-producing centre reached a peak during the second half of the 17thC, but began to decline thereafter with the growth of Delft (see pp.98-101).

Types of ware
* As well as the production of tiles and flatware, early Netherlands output included wall plaques, apothecaries' wares, bowls, bottles, vases and figures.
* Figures, and tea and coffee wares made during the 16th and 17thC are now extremely scarce in the market place.

A Dutch Delft wall plaque, c.1750-60;
ht 13¼in (33.5cm); value code F

Identification checklist for 18thC polychromatic Delft wares
1. Is the piece tin-glazed?
2. Does the item feature a blue and white design?
3. Has the design been outlined in black?
4. Does the palette also include a greyish and irregular green, a dry-looking, slightly-raised red, black, an intense egg-yellow, a greenish-turquoise or a manganese-brown?
5. Are the colours strong and bright?
6. Is the base covered in glaze with a great many "pin-holes"?
7. Is the base marked with initials or a device?

Delft
The Chinese influence on early 17thC pottery in the Netherlands (see pp. 96-7), coincided so neatly with the rise of the town of Delft as a European pottery centre, that the name has become synonymous with Oriental-style Dutch blue and white wares.

This success was due to three main factors:
* the town's coastal position in the south west of the country
* local graphic artists whose

work provided sources for designs on more sophisticated wares
* inexpensive premises in the form of disused breweries (vacant owing to the decline in the Dutch brewing trade).

Factories
The first tin-glazed pottery was established in Delft in 1584, but it was not until c.1650 that there is evidence of a boom in the town's industry, and Delft pottery took on a style of its own. The

number of master-potters listed in records of the Guild of St. Luke in Delft, founded in 1611, more than doubled to 20. From about this time marks appear, either the initials of the factory owner or the name of the factory itself – for example, *De metale Pot* (The Metal Pot), *De Roos* (The Rose), *De 3 Klokken* (The Three Bells) and *De Paauw* (The Peacock). In all there were 37 potteries in Delft, some specializing in tile production, while others, such as *De Grieksche* A (The Greek A), appeared to concentrate on higher quality tableware and decorative items.

Frederick van Frytom (1632-1702)

Among the most accomplished technicians of blue and white tin-glaze painting, Frederick van Frytom of Delft produced some highly skilled work.

His designs are characterized by detailed, dark-toned foregrounds that merge into lighter hued middle-grounds, with hazy backgrounds.

Van Frytom's work is known, not only from signed oil paintings, but also from a signed rectangular plaque. Most of his known output consists of white-bordered plates such as this one above from c.1670.

Delft polychrome wares

By the beginning of the 18thC, manufacturers in Delft seemed keen to broaden their palette. *Grand-feu* wares, such as the wall plaque in the main picture, featured iron-red and gilding. Some pieces were painted with *petit-feu* colours, including vermilion, crimson and rose-pink. This was partly due to the arrival of the brilliant multi-coloured Japanese wares, especially the bold, brocade style of Imari.

* The growing popularity of porcelain in the 18thC led to highly-elaborate pottery designs, such as the plaque in the main picture.
* Note how the blue washed areas are "trekked" or outlined in black – this characterizes a good deal of the Delft ware in the later 17th and 18thC.

Boldly decorated in the Imari style, with red and blue dominating the palette, this metal-mounted ewer has been made in the typical Dutch-Oriental style.
* This piece was made at *De Grieksche A*, and the initials of the owner, Adriaenus Koeks, appear on the back.

Drug jars

A large number of wet and dry drug jars were made in Delft in the 17th and 18thC.

Made in the late 17thC, this jar is typical of *Het Bijltje* ("The Axe") or *De witte Starre* ("The White Star").
* Made without covers, the copper lid on this piece was probably added in the 19thC.

Rococo-style Delft ware

In the second quarter of the 18thC there was a move towards rococo ornament and more romantic French inspired themes. A greater use of moulds allowed more complex forms in keeping with the fashion of the time. Fine and intricate pieces were made in relatively small quantities compared with the huge output of run-of-the-mill blue and white.

One of the elements of the rococo style was an interest in *trompe l'oeil* – the use of images or items designed to deceive the eye, such as the tureen above, made during the second half of the 18thC. Manufacturers throughout Europe produced a wide range of these ceramic fantasies, especially vessels for the dinner table, including plates with imitation fruit and vegetables, and tureens in the form of rabbits, geese or even boars' heads.

* The tureen bears the axe-shaped mark of *Het Bijltje* ("The Hatchet" factory).

Figures

Following the tradition of the great French factory at Strasbourg, many European potters copied their highly successful models of birds and animals.
* Dutch examples of models are generally not as large or as crisply-made as the majority of Strasbourg figures.
* Most Delft modelled wares are not as sensitively-coloured and detailed as the French type, which are usually painted in *petit-feu* enamels as opposed to the Dutch *grand-feu*.

This pair of polychrome Delft figures of ducks below, were made c.1775. The bright colours: yellow, blue, manganese and green, are typical of *grand-feu* enamels.

The potters of Delft produced a
great number of models of cows,
some undecorated or painted in
cold, unfired colours, others, like
this pair from the mid-18thC,
with gaily-flowered caparisons. It
has been suggested that the powerful Butcher's Guild of Delft
bedecked their finest beasts with
garlands of flowers on feast days.
Elaborately-decorated figures
such as these were probably
made for presentation.
* Note that the flowers repre-
sented are chrysanthemum
and peony, both of Asian origin
and probably borrowed from
imported Oriental porcelain.

Other forms

A range of modelled wares were
produced in Delft.
* Faience shoes are believed to
have been invented in Delft and
were popular for a long time.
* Parrots were widely produced,
adapted from designs found on
Chinese porcelain.

* Other animal figures include
monkeys, horses, goats, frogs,
cocks, hens, and tortoises such as
the one above c.1760.

Collecting

When collecting Delft animal figures, it is important to be aware
that reproductions were made in
the late 19thC. These often
include faked marks such as the
"AK" or "PAK" device of *De
Grieksche A*.

* Busts, such as this Levantine
man and woman made during the
late 18thC are also found.

Late 18thC wares

The forms and styles outlined
above continued up to the end of
the 18thC when the production
of Dutch Delft ware, faced with
competition from European
porcelain, and Josiah Wedgwood's
inexpensive creamware which
affected the output of almost all
European tin-glaze pottery, went
into decline.

Marks

Early Netherlands material is
rarely marked, certainly factory
marks do not exist much before
the end of the 17thC.
   Once they became well-
established the factories of Delft
began to use and to register their
own pottery marks. They are
usually comprise a group of
initials representing the owner of
the factory, or a device, such as
an axe for *Het Bijltje* ("The
Hatchet" factory), or bells for *De
3 Klokken* ("The Three Bells"
factory).
* Most marks are found on 18thC
pieces, usually inscribed in
cobalt-blue, although a few are
found in iron-red.

GERMAN
STONEWARE I

Siegburg armorial pewter-mounted schnelle by Hans Hilger
c.1570-80; ht 10⅝in (27cm); value code E.

Identification checklist for late 16thC Siegburg
tankards (*schnelle*)
1. Is the tankard made from fine white paste?
2. Does it have a slender, tapered form?
3. Is it bound around the base and mouth with
raised ribs?
4. Is the base slightly convex?
5. Does the decoration comprise applied, moulded
designs?
6. Does the decoration feature a coat of arms, Biblical
figures or allegorical figures?
7. Is the tankard marked?

Siegburg
Situated on the Rhine, the
potteries of Siegburg were active
in the Middle Ages, but did not
produce their best wares until the
second half of the 16thC. An almost
pure white paste distinguishes
Siegburg from other German
stonewares. The potteries declined
in the 17thC, and after the sacking
of the town by Swedish troops
in 1632 never fully recovered.
Production was monopolized
by a small number of families.

Raeren
Stonewares appear to have been
made in Raeren near Aachen
(Aix-la-Chapelle) on the Rhine
from the 15thC, but it was not
until the late 16thC that their
finest pieces were produced.
Intricate architectural vessels
composed of greyish stoneware and
covered in an iron-brown or
sometimes paler saltglaze were
made. From c.1587 a finer, greyish-
bodied material that allowed more
elaborate moulding was also used.

Made c.1600, this piece from Raeren is decorated in shallow moulded relief with dancing figures (*bauerntanz*), based on engravings by artist Hans Sebald Beham, and were a popular motif.
* The potteries declined in the later 17thC, and produced simple, everyday tavern wares until the late 19thC.

Schenkkrug

In the last quarter of the 16thC. the potters of Siegburg and Raeren began to make extremely complicated vessels.

Made in Siegburg, this jug (*schenkkrug*) dated 1601, is a more complex example than the piece shown above, is a good example of this type of ware. It is constructed in an almost architectural fashion, with the sides rising upwards in sections, apparently bolted together.
* Sandwiched between bands of formal repeated motifs, the main theme of soldiers is set in a frieze of small arcades, a favourite decorative framework.

* The rounded shoulders are decorated with a ground of diagonal cross-cutting termed *kerbschnitt*, which was used on pieces from Raeren and Westerwald, as well as Siegburg.

Schnelle

Schnelle are tall, tapered ale tankards with small handles attached towards the top of the body of the vessel. The example in the main picture is typical. It is applied with three rectangular panels of maidens bearing the arms of Saxony, Bavaria and Brandenburg.
* *Schnelle* are usually bound around the base and mouth with raised ribs; this characteristic feature reveals that the form originated from wooden tankards bound with hoops.
* The base is slightly convex; 19thC fakes tend to be flat.
* Apart from coats-of-arms, other popular subjects include allegorical or Biblical figures.

This Siegburg *schnelle* from c.1560 is marked "F. Trac", a potter who was probably employed in the workshops of Anno Knütgen from c.1559-68.
* As well as the Knütgens, the other important potting families from Siegburg were the Siemmens, the Flachs (or Vlachs) and the Oems (or Omians).

Decoration

The characteristic moulded relief designs found on Siegburg and Raeren wares often include the following:
* detailed, scrolling foliage
* masks
* fantastic or mythical creatures
* animals
* religious figures
* themes from contemporary engravings.

GERMAN STONEWARE II

A Westerwald tankard (kugelbauchkrug), late 17th or early 18thC; ht 8in (20.3cm); value code G

Identification checklist for late 17thC Westerwald wares
1. Does the piece have a glaze with an "orange-skin" effect?
2. Is the clay grey in colour?
3. Does the piece have a bulbous body?
4. Is the piece decorated with blue (and possibly manganese) detailing?
5. Is there geometric decoration or scrolling foliage in low trailed relief?
6. Is there a pewter mount?
7. If so, is it dated?

Cologne and Frechen

Among the largest producers of stoneware from the Middle Ages, the potters of Cologne and Frechen produced their best wares between c.1520 and c.1610. Owing to a dispute between the authorities of Cologne and the potters, the industry relocated during the 1590s to the nearby town of Frechen, where production continued.

The mug, *right*, from c.1530-40, has been moulded with the figures of Adam and Eve, one of the earliest subjects found on

German stoneware, here based on an engraving by Virgil Solis. Rectangular panels were cast in independent moulds before being applied to the sides of the vessel – gouge marks left by the tool used to effect this are visible on the edges of these panels.

* The stippled, "orange-peel" surface of the lustrous bronze/brown glaze is characteristically thin or patchy in places.

Bellarmines (*bartmannkrug*)

Cologne and Frechen are noted for handsome bellarmines (*bartmannkrug*), or jugs decorated with a bearded mask on the narrow neck. They have a greyish body and are covered in a characteristic iron-brown, "tiger skin" glaze which has a dappled appearance.

* The characteristic honey colour was produced by throwing salt into the kiln.

In the 16thC, bellarmines had extremely bulbous, low bodies such as this example from Cologne c.1540, with applied scrolling oak leaves and acorns. By the 17thC the form became less compressed and less stable, and the mask decoration more stylized.

Westerwald

Situated between Cologne and Frankfurt-am-Main on the Rhine, Westerwald was a major pottery producing area from the Middle Ages. The area is especially noted for hollow wares made from about 1590 until the beginning of the 19thC.

* The early wares are similar in form and decoration to Siegburg and Raeren but from the middle of the 17thC made its famous grey wares with blue and sometimes manganese detailing.

* The jug in the main picture is probably the most popular form of Westerwald vessel. It usually appears with formal scrolling foliage in low trailed slip relief covering all or part of the main bulbous body, sometimes encircling a royal English monogram either WR (William III), AR (Anne) or GR (George I, II or III). Made in Germany, these wares were often made for export to England, and this type of embellishment was very popular.

This jug or *enghalskrug* (c.1665-70) is another common form found in Rhenish and Dutch pottery, and has a generous egg-shaped body and narrow neck (the term *enghalskrug* means "narrow necked jug"). This piece has a typical thin, "orange-skin" glaze over a greyish body.

* The formal geometric decoration characterizes later 17thC Westerwald, as does the leonine mask, and the cobalt and manganese coloration.

Mounts

* A considerable number of German pottery hollow wares were mounted in pewter, sometimes stamped or incised with a date. However, it is important to be cautious because the date probably stands for the year in which the foundry supplying the mount was established, and may conflict with the date of the pottery.

* Another problem is when old vessels are fitted with later, replacement mounts which can again lead to confusion.

GERMAN
STONEWARE III

A pewter mounted armorial Kreussen tankard, dated 1689; ht 6¾in (17.5cm); value code D

Identification checklist for 17thC Kreussen wares
1. Is the piece a *humpen* (tankard or mug) with a squat shape (other forms are more unusual)?
2. Does the piece have a light brownish/olive-grey body?
3. Is the piece covered with chocolate-brown saltglaze?
4. Does the body feature enamelled colours over relief decoration?
5. If the decoration includes figures, are they the Apostles or huntsmen, or do they symbolize planets?
6. Is the piece dated?

Kreussen
Kreussen, near Bayreuth in Bavaria, is noted for its brown glazed stoneware, often detailed in bright enamel colours. Indeed these wares were the first pottery to be decorated in such colours. The best period is the 17thC when tankards and flasks decorated with popular contemporary themes were made (see below). Production appears to have ceased in the 1730s.

Features
Kreussen wares are usually characterized by:
* a light brownish or olive-grey body
* chocolate-brown saltglaze which is generally lustrous but occasionally matte.

Decoration
The twelve Apostles were one of the more popular decorative themes employed at Kreussen;

other themes included the Planets, with symbolic figures and hunting scenes. Almost always these figure subjects appear in relief decoration, heightened in bold, simple enamel colours. The main design is invariably set between narrow borders moulded in a rope-twist style, scrolling fruit or interrupted palm-like foliage.
* The correct term for a tankard decorated with the Apostles, such as the piece in the main picture, is *Apostelhumpen*.

"Thumb prints"

A feature of German stoneware are the distinctive markings found on the base of items that resemble a thumb-print. This is caused when the object is removed by string from the potter's wheel.

This effect is clearly seen on the base of this *bartmannkrug* that is dated 1607.

Annaberg and Altenburg

Potters in Annaberg and Altenburg in Saxony produced mainly jugs and tankards during the 18thC.

Annaberg produced enamelled brown wares similar to those

made in Kreussen, but most were produced about 50 years later.

In colouring Annaberg is similar to Kreussen and in some cases can be mistaken for the latter. However, generally Annaberg wares have a livelier appeal and this jug (*birnkrug*) from the late 17thC is a fine example. The ground colour is a deep bitter chocolate colour with a lustrous appearance, and is darker and less matte than Kreussen. The potter or decorator has created movement in the design with his swirling diagonal ferns, a feature of Annaberg. The enamelled palette is identical to Kreussen.

Cylindrical tankards were made in every zone of Germany, both in stoneware and in tin-glazed earthenware. This Altenburg cylindrical tankard (*walzenkrug*) c.1730, is a distinctive type from Saxony decorated in relief on a pale, yellowish rust-coloured ground.
* While small stamped motifs are found on many stonewares, the applied beaded decoration which resembles crewel work is characteristic of this town.

Collecting

With few exceptions, 18thC stoneware is more mechanical and cursorily decorated than older pieces, but compared to 19thC pieces it has undoubted (and collectable) charm. It is possible to put together a good representative collection of late 17thC and 18thC German stoneware for a relatively small outlay, even in today's market.

GERMAN FAÏENCE 1

A Nuremberg cylindrical tankard (Walzenkrug), mid-18thC; ht 10in (25.4cm); value code H

Identification checklist for 18thC German faïence
1. Is the piece made from a warm, brownish, sand-coloured material?
2. Does the base have no footrim?
3. Is the base slightly concave?
4. Is the glaze irregular (it may cover the whole of the piece or it may be patchy)?
5. Is the piece moderately-thickly potted?
6. If the piece is polychrome, is the palette dominated by blue and manganese (red, green and blue may also appear)?

Early German faïence
Apart from a few rare pieces of German maiolica that were probably made in Nuremberg in the 16thC, and at Hamburg in the early 17thC, the first major factories to manufacture tin-glazed earthenware were established in Germany in the 1660s. The pottery at Hanau was established by Daniel Behagel and his brother-in-law Jacob Van de Walle in 1661. At nearby Frankfurt, a French potter, Johann Simonet, set up a pottery in 1666. Both factories produced wares based on (and intended to compete with) Delft wares.

Frankfurt and Hanau
If there is a difference between Frankfurt and Hanau it lies in the slightly cleaner or whiter material of the former factory, and the sometimes more ambitious wares washed over in clear, lead-glaze varnish. This greater refinement probably indicates a more sophisticated market in Frankfurt.

Decoration

Early wares were mainly inspired by blue and white Chinese export porcelain decorated in the late Ming, compartmentalized *kraakporselein* style, or in the "Transitional" style (featuring garden scenes and robed figures), see on the lobed dish or *buckelplatte* below. Less common are pieces painted with portraits, armorials or biblical or other narrative subjects, the latter type often enclosed within a border of dense scrolling foliage.

* Popular at Hanau, was a style known as *Vögelsdekor*, that included birds and insects set on a ground of scattered flowers, ferns and florets.

* A few pieces are decorated in manganese-brown, yellow and green, rather than the conventional blue and white.

This form of narrow-necked jug or *enghalskrug* first appeared in c.1660, both in Holland and Germany. This late 17thC example was made in Frankfurt.

* The German version tends to have a more bulbous form than its Dutch contemporary, and often has a rope twist handle (although occasionally handles are plain).

* The original pottery handle on the piece shown above has been replaced by a metal one.

* Although 17thC hollow wares are now relatively rare, the *enghalskrug* was a popular form.

Later 17thC factories

Other faience factories were established in the latter half of the 17thC. Two were set up by Dutch potters in Berlin, one by Pieter Van der Lee in 1678, and a second by Cornelius Funcke in 1699. The early products of both concerns echo the Dutch-Oriental style that was current in the late 17th and early 18thC, in both hollow and flatwares.

* Berlin wares are made from a distinctive reddish clay, and are covered with a thin, pale-blue coloured glaze.

Other wares

Most surviving pieces from the 17thC and early 18thC are flatwares, particularly boldly lobed dishes with deep sunken centres. Known as *buckelplatte*, they are based on contemporary brass or silver originals.

* A typical blue and white example from Frankfurt is shown in the picture below. Other wares are less common, but also shown here are a Nuremburg covered dish, a sugar caster from Munden, and a pair of candlesticks from Kellinghusen.

The *walzenkrug* is one of the most characteristic wares in German pottery. The pieces in this group, all made during the mid to late 18thC in different areas of Germany, all exhibit the same basic characteristics.

* The piece on the right from Proskau, c.1780-90, is painted in low-fired (*petit-feu*) enamels in a palette similar to the one found on wares from Strasbourg in France. Simple figure subjects with no frame were popular on late 18th or early 19thC German and Austrian faience. Faience was not produced in Proskau after 1793.

* Both made during the mid-18thC, the *walzenkrug* on the left, from Magdeburg, and the

piece in the centre from Dorotheenthal, are relatively inexpensive, and represent a good way to begin a collection of German faience.

18thC German faience

In the 18thC there was a proliferation of factories throughout Germany, although the concentration was in the southern and central regions. In all there were over 80 centres of production making a variety of useful and decorative items both in *grand-feu* and *petit-feu* enamel colours.

* As the century advanced, the Chinese-Delft influence was gradually replaced by the development of a native style.

Mounts

Inscribed and dated 1730, this rare Nuremburg *walzenkrug* has been painted in enamel colours with a highly-detailed scene that features, among other figures, Martin Luther (c.1483-1546), the leader of the Reformation in Germany.

* The importance of this particular *walzenkrug* is shown by the silver-gilt mounts on the cover, and around the foot.

* The more usual material for mounts was pewter, as seen on the three *walzenkrug* above, supplied by local foundries which specialized in producing mounts for ceramics.

Forms tended to become taller and more elegant, charting the change from weighty baroque to lighter rococo.
* Made in Magdeburg c.1755, the vase above has been painted to simulate basket weave, and features a rococo-style cartouche surrounding a figure of a musician.
* The base of this vase is marked in green with an "M", a mark that is also used at Munden.

Influences
* The influence of contemporary porcelain on 18thC German faience is evident in both the form and the painting on the vase above: the *grand-feu* colours have been applied very delicately in the style of porcelain.
* Engravings by German artists were another important influence in the second and third quarters of the 18thC.

Marks
A fair proportion of German faience is marked, sometimes with the full name of the town such as "Hanau" and "Göggingen".

Sometimes the initials of the proprietor of a facory appear. The factory at Bayreuth was managed by different people.The "B.K" seen above stands for Bayreuth, Knöller), "B.P" (for Bayreuth, Pfeiffer) is also found.

Sometimes the marks of potters or faience decorators, or their workshops are found, painted on the base of their pieces.

Found on faience from Nuremburg, the marks shown above were used by faience painter Georg Friedrich Kordenbusch (d.1763) and his pupils.
* The best work by Kordenbusch includes figures on tankards, and floral and landscape decoration.
* Other marks used on German faience included devices, such as the wheel of Mainz representing the Hochst factory. This mark should not be confused with the 19thC Damm pottery in Aschaffenburg which made reproductions of Hochst porcelain. The mark on these wares features a letter "D" below the wheel.

Decorators
Relatively few pieces of German faience are decorated by known ceramic painters. Most signed pieces come from southern German factories such as Künersberg, Schrezheim or Nuremburg. These are usually painted in enamel colours, dating from the later 17thC into the mid-18thC

Hausmaler
Independent decorators working outside the main factories, known as *Hausmaler*, were employed to decorate a number of pieces of German faience. One well-known example is Abraham Helmhack (1654-1724), an engraver and glass painter who was also skilled at working on faience. His work is typified by the use of a subtle, pastel, polychrome palette, dominated by pink, pale greens and blues. He painted historical and landscape subjects, within bold, foliate borders.
* These decorators also worked on contemporary glass, using thinly-applied black and iron-red enamels, to create a style known as *schwarzlot*. Detailed landscape subjects or town scenes were popular on these pieces.

BRITISH & IRISH POTTERY

Detail from a "Midnight Modern Conversation" punch bowl, Liverpool c.1750

The manufacture of tin-glazed earthenware in England probably began with the arrival in 1567 of two Flemish potters, Jaspar Andries and Jacob Janson. According to Stow's Survey of London they "came away from Antwerp, to avoid the Persecution there, and settled themselves in Norwich … making Gally Paving Tiles, and Vessels for Apothecaries". "Gally" in an archaic term for tin-glazed earthenware such as tiles and domestic vessels. The "Vessels for Apothecaries" were doubtless alabarelli (tall dry drug jars of waisted cylindrical form) and spouted syrup pots. Andries set up a pottery in Norwich which survived to the end of the century, while Janson moved to London where he established a pottery at Aldgate to the east of the City. From old records it is clear that there were other Netherlandish potters in London at the end of the 16thC but whether they practised their art is impossible to say. By the 17thC the manufacture of tin-glazed (in this early phase the material is usually referred to as English maiolica) had spread to Southwark and Lambeth on the south bank of the Thames. London potters carried their craft to Brislington (Avon) in c.1650 and to Bristol in 1683 or slightly later. Many of those involved in the industry were from abroad, often from the Netherlands, with names that became anglicized (e.g. Janson changed to Johnson) in the parish records. This human interchange (there were English potters working in Delft) sometimes causes difficulties in distinguishing Dutch from English tin-glazed pottery, particularly before the middle of the 17thC.

Like the Dutch, there are Italian influences on the early wares, and the adoption of the Chinese style happened at around the same time, in the first half of the 17thC. The Chinese influence is felt, if at times diluted, almost until the close of the industry at the turn of the 18thC.

Among the most idiosyncratic of English delftwares is the "blue-dash" group of large dishes or chargers. They are painted with a variety of subjects including: tulips, oak-leaves, geometrical patterns, biblical themes, portraits of English monarchs or generals. Whatever the subject they are all painted in a simple but vigorous manner within a flattened rim embellished with dashes which gives rise to the title. This group spans a period of a little over a century until about 1740 when chargers seem to disappear altogether. Rarer specimens in this group have realised over six figures at auction but humbler and more battered pieces can be obtained for relatively modest sums.

There were almost a dozen potteries in and around London active in the 17thC making tin-glazed earthenware. From here in the tradition spread in the late 17thC and early 18thC to other parts of the British Isles and Eire – to Brislington, Bristol, Wincanton, Liverpool, Glasgow and Dublin. While it is possible to attribute some pieces to particular towns, in many cases it is difficult to distinguish London ware from that made in Bristol or Liverpool in the 18thC. The material, with some slight variations, is the same and one tends to rely more on the decoration and on the patterns on the undersides of dishes for attribution. This is not an accurate science, as potters and designs dispersed widely, causing great confusion in the study of ceramics. However, because of the wealth of dated English delftware, it is at least possible to follow the changing styles with some success. In general, there is a subtle process of refinement in the material, especially the glaze which, by the middle of the 18thC, is smooth and satin-like.

After about 1720 British and Irish delftware is not easily confused with any of its Continental rivals. Designs have a character of their own, whether they are Oriental or European in inspiration. A slight allowance may be made for the Dublin factory of Henry Delamain, whose wares often have a Continental feel.

Throughout the 18thC English delftware continued to embrace the use of Chinoiserie. Even in scenes which are supposedly English, there is often a flavour of Orientalism. By and large, the Chinoiseries of the 18thC adopt a less literal interpretation than their 17thC predecessors. The relatively large-scale "Transitional" style meditative figures are eschewed in favour of smaller scale landscapes with fanciful riverside pagodas and pavilions, and if there are figures they are decidedly eccentric. Chinese flower patterns are also popular and are given a loose informal treatment much in keeping with contemporary Chinese export porcelain.

Staffordshire has enjoyed a pre-eminent position in international ceramics from the latter half of the 18thC, although its tradition goes back for centuries. The area is fortunate in having rich deposits of different clays, ample supplies of cheap fuel from local coalmines and a good system of waterways to transport their products around England. North Staffordshire is the location of the largest pottery factories in England, mainly based in or around the "Five Towns" – Burslem, Hanley, Longton, Stoke and Tunstall – simply known as The Potteries. It is here that many of the best-known types of pottery were produced – slipware, agate ware, redware, creamware (including Prattware), pearlware, jasper, black basaltes and saltglazed stoneware. Some of the most celebrated names in ceramics practised their craft here – Thomas Toft, John Astbury, Thomas Whieldon, Josiah Spode and Josiah Wedgwood.

The output of the Staffordshire potteries in the 17thC consisted almost entirely of lead-glazed pottery, although stoneware was produced in the last few years of the century. In the early 18thC stoneware took over as the major product, first with simple scratched and applied moulded decoration, and from about 1740, with completely-moulded objects such as teapots, tea caddies and dishes.

In the middle years of the 18thC fine quality, multi-coloured lead-glazed pottery wares and figures were made by Thomas Whieldon, Josiah Wedgwood and others. These in turn were supplanted by creamware, first invented by Enoch Booth of Tunstall, but refined and brilliantly marketed by Josiah Wedgwood. This ware was so successful that it was copied extensively on the Continent. Wedgwood was also responsible for making some of Staffordshire's most refined and influential stonewares: his Neo-classical black basaltes and jasper wares are instantly recognizable.

In the 19thC Staffordshire is virtually synonymous with both blue and white transfer-printed earthenware tablewares pioneered by Josiah Spode and whose efforts spawned numerous imitators both here and later in the United States. There was also a considerable market in figures both of a general decorative nature with romantic shepherds and other pastoral figures set among flowering branches and continuing the late 18thC tradition, animals and neo-classical portrait busts of notables, including Nelson and Bonaparte. Towards the middle of the century a new type of ceramic sculpture arrived, the so-called 'flatbacks' figures and groups produced in what was essentially a cottage industry, mainly for relatively humble households of the time. Made in huge quantities many reflect the social and political history of the latter 19thC with figures or groups of Crimean soldiers, famous circus acts or even murderers. Nowadays they are eagerly sought by collectors, especially in the English-speaking world.

The first half of the 19thC was a period of immense change in the potteries of England, a transitional phase during which the relatively small world dominated by the potter-craftsman, was taken over by large-scale, industrial operations. In part, Josiah Wedgwood was responsible for this, introducing systematic procedures and removing much from the hands of individual potters. Production became mechanized and slick, and lacked much spontaneity.

The middle years of the 19thC are among the bleakest in pottery history with little innovation or inspiration. Around the Great Exhibition of 1851 when the swelling numbers of the middle classes discovered the aristocratic tastes of former times. The insatiable demand for replicas, reproductions and pastiches of the classic wares of the Renaissance and the Baroque ensured that the larger and more sophisticated manufacturers such as Minton were working at full capacity. Apart from their vast range of Sèvres style porcelains, Minton developed a type of pottery termed "majolica" (the word is a corruption of maiolica, which it does not resemble in the least), an intricately-modelled and generally large-scale ware, dressed mostly in sombre heavy colours.

The backlash of the Arts and Crafts Movement towards the end of the century was a recognition of this lack of individuality. Henry Doulton, himself an industrial producer, initiated a reappraisal of the potter and his role during this period by collaborating with the students of the Lambeth School of Art in south London to produce a group of hand-thrown stonewares, which were decorated by leading artists. A number of individuals, including the Martin Brothers, William De Morgan and William Moorcroft, became prominent and reintroduced some life-force to the potting world. They all contributed to a move away from mass-production, making what has become known as Art Pottery. Reinforcing this drive towards individuality, was the arrival of Japanese decorative and graphic arts following the opening-up of the country at the end of the 19thC, and also the increased awareness of material from the Islamic world. The inspiration of the exotic is evident, if subtle, in much of the best work of the late 19thC.

The 20thC saw the rise of the Studio potter, a craftsman or woman who modelled or turned, glazed, decorated and fired his or her own wares. Bernard Leach is probably the best-known of the early Studio potters, and his Chinese and Japanese-influenced pieces are widely collected, together with those of his colleague Shoji Hamada. William Staite Murray and Michael Cardew are other key figures. Modern, post-War ceramics are dominated by the work of Dame Lucie Rie and Hans Coper. These two potters worked closely togteher for many years, experimented widely with forms, glazes and materials, and produced highly indivdual wares that have become very popular.

BRITISH & IRISH CENTRES

It is not certain where the first characteristic British pottery, which appeared during the 14thC, was produced, but is is likely that many of the finer wares were made in monasteries. In the 15th and 16thC, green-glazed jugs and hard, red, brown-glazed wares were made.

During the 16th and 17thC glazed, relief-moulded slipwares were produced in Staffordshire (especially in the area around Burslem), and at Wrotham in Kent. A highly skilled technique, many Studio potters in the late 19th and early 20thC attempted to imitate the style. The most notable of these being Bernard Leach at his pottery in St. Ives in Cornwall, and Michael Cardew.

Tin-glazed earthenware ware first appeared in Britain in the mid-16thC, in London and Norwich. Lambeth in south London was one of the principal centres, but other areas also made these early tin-glazed wares, known as "Gallyware". These potteries were based in Aldgate in east London, and Southwark on the south banks of the River Thames. The production of delftware in London continued well into the 18thC. Potters from London were responsible for the spread of English delftware to many other parts of the country.

Other major centres were Bristol, Wincanton, Liverpool, Glasgow and Dublin. There is evidence of a factory at Delftfield in Glasgow, 1748-1810 (records show that 60,000-80,000 pieces were exported per year), but there are very few identifiable wares. The Wincanton pottery ran for about 20 years, c.1730-50, and some inscribed and dated pieces have been found. Bristol was a very important centre, although many of the early wares were made at Brislington, a couple of miles outside the city. The first dated piece from Brislington was made in 1649, and production of delftwares in Bristol began after 1683. Stonewares and earthenwares were also made in this area. Delftware was first produced in Liverpool c.1710. By 1730 there were at least four potteries in the city, and production continued until the late 18thC, when the commercial and technical success of Josiah Wedgwood's creamwares (see pp.136-7) forced them out of business. This fate also befell delftware potteries in other parts of the country.

Staffordshire rose to prominence during the 18thC, with a large number of pottery towns (see facing page). Output included salt-glazed stonewares, lead-glazed wares, originally produced by Thomas Whieldon at Fenton Low, redwares, polychrome wares and creamwares. Josiah Wedgwood also developed a range of new products such as jasper ware and black basaltes. Other 18th and 19thC centres included Leeds, Derby and Liverpool.

Belfast

Dublin

St Ives

Staffordshire
Since the early 17thC, Staffordshire has been the centre of the English ceramics industry. Based around the town of Stoke-on-Trent, important pottery towns and areas include Tunstall, Burslem, Cobridge, Hanley, Fenton, Lane Delph, Lane End, Longton, Longport, Shelton and Newcastle-under-Lyme.

Josiah Wedgwood, in partnership with Thomas Bentley, built a pottery and a village on a site two miles from Burslem that opened in 1769. They called the area Etruria, a name inspired by ancient Etruscan pottery, which also influenced some of the factory's new products, such as ornamental vases in the Classical style, portrait busts, medallions and clock cases.

Greenock ▲

Glasgow ▲ Edinburgh ▲

Newcastle ▲

Sunderland ▲

Liverpool ▲

Burslem ▲ Stoke ▲

STAFFS

Nottingham ▲

Coalport ▲

Norwich ▲

Birmingham ▲

London ▲

Bristol ▲

Wrotham ▲

117

ENGLISH
DELFTWARE 1

A rare English delftware charger, c.1670-80
ht 13in (33cm); value code A

Identification checklist for 17thC "blue-dash" chargers
1. Does the piece have a flattened rim painted with blue dashes?
2. Is the design simple yet lively?
3. Does the subject include tulips, oak leaves, geometric patterns, a biblical theme, or a portrait of an English monarch or general?
4. Is the brushwork crude and vigorous?
5. Is the foot thickly cut, perhaps with a small hole?
6. Is the back of the piece covered with a brownish, translucent "varnish"?
7. If the piece is an item of flatware, is there a weal (½in, 1.3cm in length) under the outer rim (see p.120)?

16th and 17thC English maiolica and delftware

The manufacture of tin-glazed earthenware in England probably began with the arrival in 1567 of two Flemish potters, Jaspar Andries and Jacob Janson. According to Stow's Survey of London they "settled themselves in Norwich ... making Gally Paving Tiles, and Vessels for Apothecaries". The term "Gallyware" was used to describe tin-glazed pottery.

Manufacturers

Andries set up a pottery in Norwich which survived to the end of the 16thC. Janson moved to London

where he established a pottery at Aldgate, to the east of the City of London. By the 17thC the manufacture of tin-glazed pottery had spread to other centres in London, and to Bristol (c.1683). This early material is usually referred to as English maiolica.

Styles

Although Dutch and English tin-glazed earthenware both derive from 16thC Antwerp, there is a noticeable divergence in style from the beginning of the 17thC.
* Around 90 per cent of English delftware is blue and white, painted in the Chinese style.

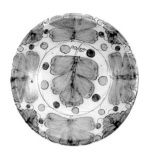

blue dashes around the rim –
hence the name – they are
painted with a variety of subjects
including:
* tulips
* oak-leaves
* geometrical patterns
* biblical themes
* portraits of English monarchs
or generals.
The design on the piece in the
main picture is unusual – animal
designs are not commonly used,
but the style of the painting is
distinctly English.

* Other English wares tend to
be simple and robust, eschewing
detail for a lively and spontaneous
hand. Patterns are relatively
primitive, the decorator relying
on simple repeating motifs or
patterns, seen on the oak leaf
charger above.
* Dutch pottery can be architectural and intricate, and the
decoration is usually more
considered: good examples are
pieces by Frederik van Frytom
and of Adriaenus Koeks' *De
Grieksche A* factory (see pp.98-9).

Influences
Italian influences are clear on
early delftwares in the first half of
the 17thC, and the adoption
of the Chinese style happens
at around the same time. The
Chinese influence continued
until almost the end of the
decorative delft industry in
England at the turn of the 18thC.

"Blue-dash" wares are painted in
a simple but vigorous manner
within a flattened rim embellished with dashes. This group
spans a period of a little over a
century until about 1740 when
chargers seem to disappear altogether. Rarer specimens in this
group have realized vast sums at
auction, but humbler and more
worn pieces can be obtained for
much less.
* The piece shown above features
a chequered pattern which is
probably from the Netherlands,
and pomegranates which are
Italian in style.

Decoration
The majority of 17thC English
chargers, including the example
in the main picture, are not
entirely covered in white tin-
glaze. To save on expensive
tin the back was washed in
the cheaper lead-glaze. The
effect is to produce a straw or
brownish coloured translucent
"varnish" through which the
often crude pottery body is visible. The foot is thickly cut and
wedge-shaped so that a piece
of cord can be wound around it
for suspension on a wall. Sometimes the foot-rim or the lip of
the dish was pierced with a small
hole at the time of manufacture
for display purposes.

This Chinese-style, octagonal
plate, a contemporary form used
for silver wares, was probably
made in London in the late 17thC.

"Blue-dash" wares
Among the most idiosyncratic
of English delftwares is the
"blue-dash" group of large dishes
or chargers, such as the piece in
the main picture. Decorated with

ENGLISH
DELFTWARE II

Material
While it is generally agreed that English delftware is more primitive in decoration, the material is often as smooth if not occasionally smoother than contemporary Dutch or German tin-glazed pottery. Glaze is bluish, particularly on blue and white decorated pieces, but a warm creamy tone is found on less common plain white pieces.
* Flatwares are fired on thin stilts which leave a knife-like weal about ½ in in length under the outer flange or rim.

Types of wares
A variety of useful and decorative wares were produced in the 17thC, some similar to northern European pottery – particularly Dutch and German – but others are entirely English in form.

Domestic wares
A large group of items was made for domestic use, including the following:
* *flatwares:* chargers with concave wells and narrow, bevelled rims; small plates with flat centres and relatively broader rims – based on contemporary pewter; octagonal dishes with very broad rims, the shallow centre about half the overall diameter.

The Boscobel Oak holds an important place in English Royal mythology – it was in this tree that King Charles II was alleged to have hidden from the Roundheads. This dish, probably made in Lambeth c.1710, shows the King together with three crowns and the Royal cipher.
* *caudle cups:* made in a swelling, bombé form, caudle cups were

made to hold caudle, a weak alcoholic drink composed of heated (but not boiling) wine or ale flavoured with cinnamon or other spices.

While English 17thC delftware is not marked (see below), inscriptions and dates found on some pieces such as this caudle cup which is dated 1674, give an understanding of the development of delftware. Some pieces are embellished with the arms of a company as seen here, or the initials of an individual or a married couple. Apart from the coat of arms, the rest of the cup is painted in Chinese "transitional" style, conventional decoration for the late 17thC.
* *mugs:* barrel-shaped, globular with cylindrical necks, and cylindrical form with straight sides.
* *wine cups:* usually on knopped or annulated stems.
* *fuddling cups:* comprising three (or four) small cups linked by entwined strap handles.
* *posset pots:* a favourite potion in 17th and 18thC England, posset was a concoction of milk, liquor, spices and sugar that was probably taken for minor ills. The vessels made to serve it in were bombé or cylindrical in shape with domed covers.

The bombé form of the posset pot seen above, with the double-scroll handles and serpentine spout echoing the curves of the sides, was more common than cylindrical-shaped examples. Here the decorator has broken away from the dominant oriental influence to produce a simple but effective pattern.

jugs: generally made with globular bodies and tall slender or straight necks; some are found in the form of a cat.

* *punch-bowls:* the earliest dated specimen is 1681; in the 17thC and early 18thC they were very deep, some supported on a tallish foot.

* *porringers:* small bowls with a single pierced handle.

* *wine bottles:* made in a basically globular form, these have a tall narrow neck which is either annulated or flanged at the mouth.

* *candlesticks, flower vases,* and *pierced baskets:* items clearly based on silver originals.

* *salts:* holders for salt were made in various forms, including triangular, and the capstan shape seen below. Pieces of similar form to this salt have been dated to the 1670s are recorded, but this example is from the late 17thC. The Oriental-style ornamentation is clearly debased and casually executed; earlier pieces are considerably closer to the original Chinese. Note the buff granular body showing through on the vulnerable projecting parts – the rim and on the "napkin-scrolls".

Marks

English delftware does not carry factory marks. Most attributions are based on excavated material or pieces that have been inscribed.

Other items

In addition, delftware potters made considerable quantities of tiles and pharmaceutical wares. The latter include wet-drug jars, i.e. those with spouts, and dry drug jars which are mostly ovoid, such as the one below.

* An interesting collecting area, drug jars are widely available and relatively inexpensive.

ENGLISH DELFTWARE III

A Bristol "Peacock" charger, c.1720-30;
ht 13⅜in (34cm); value code D

Identification checklist for 18thC English delftware
1. Is the glaze smooth and satin-like?
2. Is the piece dated?
3. Is the piece blue and white (polychrome wares are less common; but if polychrome, do the colours include iron-red, yellow, green, brown, manganese purple and cobalt blue)?
4. Does the decoration feature a Chinese-style design, a European scene, a biblical or commemorative subject, or an inscription?
5. If the design is Chinese, is it loose and informal?

18thC delftware
There were almost a dozen potteries in and around London active in the 17thC making tin-glazed earthenware. The tradition spread in the late 17thC and early 18thC to other parts of the British Isles – to Brislington, Bristol, Wincanton, Liverpool, Glasgow and Dublin. While it is possible to attribute some pieces to particular towns, it is difficult to distinguish London ware from Bristol or Liverpool in the 18thC. The material, with some slight variations, is the same, and identification depends more on the decoration and on the patterns on the undersides of dishes. Unfortunately this is not accurate, as both potters and designs moved around.

Marks
Although not marked by factories, a relatively large amount of 18thC English delft is dated; this helps to classify unmarked pieces and makes it possible to follow changing styles with some success.

An example of early 18thC delft, this shoe is dated 1709.
By the middle of the 18thC the material becomes gradually more refined, especially the glaze which appears smooth and satin-like.
* Pottery shoes appear to have been purely decorative and intended as gifts. Some are inscribed with the initials of husband and wife and symbols of love.

Decorative styles
After about 1720 English delftware is not easily confused with any of its Continental rivals. Designs have a character of their own, whether they are oriental or European in inspiration: patterns are looser and less complex, scenes and figures are cruder and less meticulous than those produced in mainland Europe.

All English delftware factories made puzzle jugs, such as this one produced in Bristol c.1730-40. Medieval in origin, they are found in varying forms. In the middle and later 18thC, "European" scenes became more common: low-slung cottages and simplified landscapes, such as those seen on this piece, are found on Bristol, Liverpool and London delft.
* A type of primitive decoration

peculiar to Bristol is known as "farmhouse" style, the peacock dish in the main picture is a typical example.

18thC Chinese styles
Throughout the 18thC English delftware continues in the Chinese style; even supposedly English scenes often have a sense of the Oriental. In general 18thC Chinoiseries are a less literal interpretation of original Chinese painting than their 17thC predecessors.
   Typical Chinese-style subjects include:
* fanciful riverside pagodas and pavilions
* eccentric figures
* flower and bird designs.

Although a conventional porcelain form, delftware teapots such as this one from the mid-18thC are very rare, mainly because tin-glazed earthenwares cannot tolerate hot liquids, and like most teapots in daily use are easily damaged.
* This bird design is a theme borrowed from Chinese export-ware porcelain.

Other subjects
Besides Chinese styles, the range of decoration includes:
* European landscapes
* biblical subjects
* inscribed pieces
* commemorative pieces such as cups, plates and chargers.
   The cockerel and the peacock are both popular birds found on English delftware. The peacock is often a misinterpretation of the Oriental phoenix, but the example in the main picture appears in a domestic setting among simply-sponged trees.

Colours
Blue and white wares still predominate but there are relatively more polychromatic pieces using iron-red, yellow, green, brown and a manganese purple as well as the cobalt-blue.

DELFTWARE:
OTHER CENTRES

A large dish painted in blue, Henri Delamain's factory, Dublin, c.1755; lgth 19in (48.2cm); value code F.

Identification checklist for 18thC Irish delftwares by Henri Delamain

1. Is the piece painted in blue or manganese purple (which appears almost black)?
2. Is the subject a landscape?
3. Is the painting sophisticated?
4. Is there a narrow scroll border?
5. If the piece is marked, is there an "H" in monogram with a "D", the word "Dublin" (which occasionally appears with a harp), or a painter's mark "NE"?

Delamain (Belgian, d.1757)

Henri Delamain made pottery in Dublin from 1752, although a delftware pottery had been in existence from 1734 (known from an inscription found on a Chinese-style plate). Delamain's factory was run by his wife and others after his death, and pieces were produced until at least as late as 1771.

Characteristics

The delftware attributed to Delamain is painted in bright blue or in puce/manganese purple, such as the dish in the main picture, c.1755, chiefly with landscapes and narrow scroll borders.
* The style of Delamain's painting, and the motifs used in the border are very distinctive.
* The painting has a more sophisticated European or Continental feel than any other found in the British Isles, although some items have been misattributed to Liverpool.
* Most wares are unmarked, but an "H" in monogram with a "D" refers to Delamain; "Dublin" is known, sometimes together with a harp, and a painter's mark "NE" occasionally appears.

Delftfield (est. 1748)

The Delftfield factory was founded in Glasgow by Robert Dinwoodie and operated for a very short period. Almost all attributions have been made from one punch bowl painted in blue with the arms of the city.
* Other than this small group of wares, most pottery produced in Scotland is earthenware.

Glasgow wares, such as this crested plate from c.1760, are particularly scarce. The crest belongs to an important local family. While the palette is similar to the Liverpool Fazackerly wares – a greyish green, a fox-red and an opaque white – the dotted effect around the vegetation is entirely Scottish.

* Two flower-painted mugs dated 1757 and 1758 made for Thomas Fazackerley and his wife Catherine, exist in a Liverpool museum. From these a good deal of Liverpool pottery has been identified.

Other 18thC wares

A variety of other delftwares were made during the 18thC. The acorn-shape of this double handled jar (below), c.1720-40, appears to be a form that is unique to England.

The rope-twist handles see here are found on a good deal of English pottery in the 17thC, and the first part of the 18thC.

* In common with a large number of jars made in the 18thC, the cover from this piece is missing.

* When deciding whether a piece of delftware is genuine, always look for wear on the base and the footrim which should look natural.

This English-made piece has an extremely intricate lineage. Made in c.1740, it is based on a Chinese-Imari original, in a form that was borrowed by potters in the Far East from European silverware.

* The palette is based on Japanese Imari wares, with the decoration painted in iron-red and blue.

* Original Japanese Imari wares would feature gilding, and while there is none on this English piece, a Dutch contemporary would have been gilded.

* The complexity of the knop on the lid of thius piece is typically British – it is similar to stems found on glasses made at the around the same time.

Collecting

* Flatwares are widely available and can be obtained at modest prices.

* Hollow wares are less common – daily use has meant that relatively few have survived to the present day.

* 80-90 per cent of wares are blue and white, pieces in this group can be collected at relatively low cost, especially if the item is a commonly-found form such as a piece of flatware, or is slightly damaged.

* Polychrome wares are generally worth three to four times as much as blue and white pieces.

* Pieces in perfect condition will be worth twice as much as chipped items, although it is extremely rare to find an unblemished piece of English or Continental delft.

* Wares with more complicated decoration, such as figures, can be worth four times as much as those with more usual designs.

* Dates, initials, dedications and other inscriptions, can also boost prices.

STAFFORDSHIRE SLIPWARE

A Staffordshire slipware cup, dated 1690;
ht 7in (17.8cm); value code C

Identification checklist for Staffordshire slipware
1. Does the piece have a red/buff clay body?
2. Has the piece been covered with chocolate brown and white (that appears yellow) slip?
3. Is the glaze glassy and thick?
4. Is the body slightly irregular?
5. Does the brown on the body drift into the yellow?
6. Is there trailed decoration (feathering in particular appears to be unique to Staffordshire)?

Slipware

Slipware is probably the earliest identifiable type of pottery made in Staffordshire, although it was also made elsewhere in England, most notably at Wrotham in Kent, c.1612-1710. Some inscribed and dated specimens of slipware have survived, and are eagerly sought by collectors in both Britain and the United States, where there is a strong demand for the types of wares used by early colonial settlers.

* Thomas Toft and his family made a number of inscribed wares at Burslem in Staffordshire in the 17thC.
* The slipware jug shown *right*, is a high quality piece, with a rich, golden glaze and moulded, relief decoration.

A characteristic bulbous form, posset pots such as this one c.1690, were everyday vessels. This piece has been inscribed "JOHN MARE: HIS CUP", and is a rare individualized example.
* Because of the inscription, this piece is very expensive, but an uninscribed piece with some damage could be acquired for much less.

Characteristics
Slipware is composed of secondary red or buff-coloured clay, decorated in brown and white coloured slip, which is then covered in a thick, glassy, clear lead glaze. There is a small amount of iron present in the lead glaze which gives a slightly yellowish cast to the underlying white slip. On the large footless dishes the backs are left free of glaze. Thinly potted vessels are rare, and most are thickly constructed and able to withstand domestic use.

Decoration
As well as trailed and dotted slip decoration i.e. slip poured from a spouted vessel to draw the design, sgraffiato or scratched decoration, and applied moulding were also used to decorate slipware. 18thC slipware was sometimes press-moulded with more complex designs as seen in the octagonal plate (below), some with radiating patterns of stylized flowers, or with human or animal figures.

Subjects
As well as abstract designs, favourite subjects on slipware include Adam and Eve, mermaids, cockerels, royal portraits, crests and coats of arms.

Types of wares
Slipware was clearly aimed at a relatively local market, and items include large dishes and other flatwares, honey pots, salt pigs, loving cups and other domestic vessels.

Oblong dishes such as this rectangular "Boar's Head" dish from the late 18thC, were made in large numbers in the 18thC and into the 19thC. The pattern has been "feathered" with a comb or some pointed tool, in cream coloured slip on a dark ground.
* Feathered decoration appears to be unique to Staffordshire.
* A dish of this type can be obtained relatively inexpensively.

Marks
Apart from rare pieces which are inscribed on the decorated area of the object with the maker's name, such as Thomas Toft, George and William Talor, John Wright, John Simpson, Samuel Malkin or other potters, early slipware is unmarked.

Made c.1715, this octagonal dish is signed "IS" and was probably made by John Simpson. An example of press-moulded ware, the design features alternating pomegranates and *fleurs-de-lis* around a floral design.

Collecting
* The majority of slipwares that exist today are damaged to some degree, and therefore a certain amount of chipping or cracking should be acceptable to the collector, especially at the more affordable end of the market.
* Although thickly potted, slipwares do tend to be brittle, so handle with care.

127

SALT-GLAZED STONEWARES

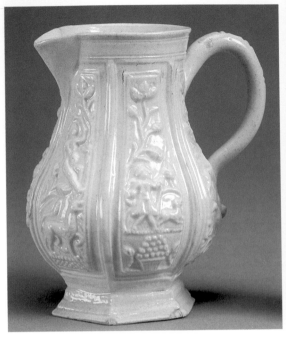

A small white salt-glazed cream jug, c.1750;
ht 3¾in (9.5cm); value code F/G

Identification checklist for 18thC salt-glazed stoneware
1. Is the material greyish-white in colour (only visible if the piece is worn)?
2. Is the piece yellowish-cream in colour?
3. Is the glaze very thin with a granular surface?
4. Does the piece have a slightly matte surface?
5. Is the piece neatly potted?
6. Is there moulded decoration?
7. If the piece has coloured decoration, is it painted in a *famille rose* palette, with pinks and turqouises?

Salt-glazed Stoneware
A potter called John Dwight patented the technique of producing salt-glazed stoneware in Britain in 1693, but the process was soon being copied by other factories. It was probably first produced in Staffordshire at the end of the 17thC by John and David Elers, who moved from

Fulham in London after London-based Dwight threatened them with legal action. The technique was then adopted by potteries throughout Staffordshire.

Techinque
Originally developed in Germany, salt-glazing involves throwing common salt into the kiln when

128

the furnace reaches its maximum temperature of 2500°F (1300-1400°C). The salt then separates into chlorine, which was passed out through the kiln chimney, and sodium, which combined with the silicates in the clay to form a thin, glass-like glaze. Salt glaze is a thin ceramic glaze, and the surface has a granular, "orange-peel" appearance.
* Salt-glazed stoneware was made in Staffordshire c.1710-70.

By the 1720s, the Staffordshire potters had refined salt-glazed stoneware to the point where it was able to compete commercially with imports of Chinese porcelain. This teapot in the form of a house from the mid-18thC, illustrates the thin, cream-coloured glaze characteristic of this type of ware.
* Staffordshire potters made many imaginative teapot forms including a camel!

Coloured decoration
* A small proportion of salt-glazed stoneware made after 1750 was decorated in coloured enamel, sometimes crudely echoing imported Chinese *famille-rose* porcelain, with pinks and turquoises.

* In the 1750s transfer-printing in overglaze black or red, seen here on this octagonal plate c.1755, was added to the decorator's repertoire.
* Salt-glazed plates are almost always moulded with trellis borders similar to this example.

Marks
Apart from a few dated master moulds and documented pieces, Staffordshire salt-glazed wares are unmarked.

Agateware
A rarer category of stoneware is "agate" ware, which was made to imitate the veined and marbled surface of the hardstone agate.

Frederick the Great, the King of Prussia was a popular figure in England during the mid-18thC, and his portrait often appears on pottery and porcelain. The blotchy, greyish-pink and the strong blue on the teapot above c.1760, comprise the usual palette for wares produced around this time.

* Solid agateware was created by pressing slabs of tinted clay together and then kneading cross-cut sections together to give a veined effect.
* A marbled effect can be achieved by blending and combing coloured slips on the surface of a piece of stoneware; this was known as "surface agateware".
* Small tewares and seated figures of cats, such as the one above c.1745, are perhaps the best-known agatewares. Agateware cats are keenly collected.

WHIELDON-TYPE WARES

A Whieldon-type tortoiseshell plate , c.1765;
dia. 10in (25.4cm); value code G/H

Identification checklist for Whieldon-type wares
1. Is the piece covered with a mottled glaze?
2. Is the glaze thick and sumptuous?
3. Is the glaze brown or green (blue and grey are occasionally found)?
4. Do the colours drift into one another?
5. Is there a slight iridescence on the surface?
6. Is the surface covered with a neat, regular crackle?
7. Is the piece thinly potted?
8. Are there spurs on the base?
9. If there is any other decoration, is it applied, such as scattered sprigs, trailing stems or foliage?

Thomas Whieldon (1719-95)
Thomas Whieldon developed his characteristic mottled, lead-glazed wares in his factory at Fenton Low, Staffordshire, c.1740-80. Josiah Wedgwood was his partner, 1754-8. His early output primarily included salt-glazed stoneware and creamware, in the form of tea services and knife and fork handles. The first examples of the new lead-glazed wares produced in the 1750s were made in shades of olive green, grey, brown and slate blue.

* Many other potteries in the area produced similar wares, and unless pieces can be positively attributed to the factory, they are described as "Whieldon-type" wares.

Characteristics
The tortoiseshell plate in the main picture is typical of Whieldon-type wares, with a characteristic thick, sumptuous, mottled glaze, with the colours drifting into one another, a thinly-potted body, and a surface covered in a neat, regular crackle.

130

* A slight iridescence on the surface, seen on this detail of the back of the plate in the main picture.
* Also visible are two or three circular spurs left by the pins that supported the plate during firing, another feature of Whieldon wares.

Decoration
Decoration on Whieldon-type wares mainly comprised applied, rustic *trompe d'oeil* motifs, such as scattered sprigs, trailing stems and foliage.

This high quality coffee pot and cover, c.1760-65, features crisply moulded relief vegetation, and a naturalistic "crabstock" handle and spout that is typical of Whieldon. The "crabstock" form is based on the gnarled branches of the crab apple tree.

Output
Whieldon produced mainly teawares in conventional Staffordshire forms (many moulds were common to many factories in the area). But some decorative items were also made.
* Excavations at Fenton Low have revealed that Whieldon's pottery made redwares, stonewares and agatewares, as well as tortoiseshell pottery, all of which have "crabstock" handles and applied vine scroll motifs.

Made c.1755, this model of a dovecote is a rare example of Whieldon-type ware. The piece is finely modelled with applied birds and a moulded roof.
* Human and animal figures were also made in this type of ware.

Cow creamers
Traditionally Thomas Whieldon is supposed to have been the first potter to manufacture cow creamers, such as the one below, c.1765-70. A form of milk jug, the cow's mouth is the spout, the tail functions as a handle, and there is a cover in the centre of its back. Made as copies of silver originals, pottery versions became quite common and were produced in Yorkshire, the north-east of England, Scotland and South Wales. Following a typhoid epidemic in the 1850s, their popularity declined as they were considered unhygienic.
* Cow creamers are eagerly collected and frequently appear at auction.

LATE 18THC & EARLY 19THC POTTERY

A "traditional" Toby Jug by Ralph Wood, c.1780; ht 9½in (24cm); value code F/G

Identification checklist for late 18thC Ralph Wood Toby jugs

1. Is the glaze smooth?
2. Can the manufacturer be positively identified (either by an impressed mark or a paper label)?
3. Are there enamel colours painted over a clear glaze?
4. Are the colours semi-transparent, not opaque?
5. If yellow is present, is it pale?
6. Are the colours, glazes and modelling high quality?
7. Is the Toby jug's tricorn hat present and in good condition?

Late 19thC English pottery

The latter half of the 18thC was dominated by the development of creamware, Prattware, and stonewares such as black basaltes, jasper and caneware.

Toby jugs

Toby jugs were based on the celebrated drinker Harry Elwes, nicknamed Toby Philpot, such as the "traditional" example in the main picture. Between 1748 and 1795 many variations of Toby jug were made, including the "Thin Man", the "Rodney's Sailor" and the "Admiral Howe".
* Look for sharply delineated, subtle enamel colours.
* Ralph Wood II made the best and most valuable Toby jugs.
* Impressed marks or labels will enhance the value of a Toby jug.

Creamware

Invented by Enoch Booth of Tunstall in the 1740s, creamware is a refined, cream-coloured earthenware, with a transparent lead glaze.

Sophisticated enough to be a substitute for porcelain, creamware was not only used to make everyday tablewares, such as the "chintz" pattern coffee pot by Wedgwood, c. 1770 (above), but also for more unusual objects – food-warmers, cruet sets and candlesticks, as well as elaborate, decorative pieces and figures.
* Although the body of creamware is as thin as porcelain, it is robust and not prone to chipping.
* Other forms of decoration include painting, and transfer printing in a wide range of subjects including landscapes, classical ruins, exotic birds, shipping scenes, portraits, coats-of-arms as well as prize fighters!
* Creamware was not only made in Staffordshire but at Leeds, Liverpool, Bristol and Swansea; it was also made in Europe and in North America.

Pearlware
In 1779 Wedgwood developed a variation on creamware which because of its slightly bluish appearance was called "Pearlware". It was used widely by manufacturers well into the 19thC, and is mainly decorated in a runny underglaze blue with chinoiserie subjects, but was sometimes decorated in Pratt-type colours (see below).

Prattware
Prattware evolved in the last quarter of the 18thC and is similar to pearlware in colour and weight. Made in Staffordshire, north-east England and in Scotland, Prattware is distinguished by a bold, high-temperature palette that comprises yellow-ochre, blue, green and muddy brown. These colours were usually used to heighten relief decoration on wares which included jugs or details on figures.

Types of Prattware include figures such as the dairyman shown above, allegorical subjects, animals, and domestic hollow wares; flatwares are rare.

Other late 18thC stonewares
* Caneware: a yellowish stoneware used for domestic wares.
* Black basaltes, jasper ware and Wedgwood's version of agate ware: mainly decorative items.

Ralph Wood wares
The Wood family, Ralph I (1715-72), and his son Ralph II (1748-95) from Burslem in Staffordshire made a series of earthenwares from c.1765, mainly figures (pastoral and animal subjects), initially decorated in rich underglaze colours similar to earlier, Whieldon-type wares. Later Wood wares were painted more carefully, keeping the coloured washes separate.

The figures in this pastoral group, c.1770-80, have plump cheeks and slightly protruding eyes that are characteristic of Wood wares.
* The blue used on Wood wares is purer than the grey tone found on Whieldon and Wedgwood pieces, and the yellow is paler.

STAFFORDSHIRE FIGURES

A Prattware portrait bust of a naval officer, c.1810-20; ht 9in (22.9cm); value code F

Identification checklist for early 19thC Prattware-type figures
1. Does the piece have a cream-coloured body?
2. Is the body relatively lightweight?
3. Is the piece decorated with underglaze colours?
4. Does the palette include a brownish ochre, dull blue and green?
5. Is the painting splashed and daubed?
6. Is the modelling crude but lively?

Late 18th and 19thC Staffordshire figures
Creamware and pearlware figures and groups were extremely popular in the late 18th and 19thC. Some of those made in the late 18thC are high quality and are relatively expensive. But by the 19thC, porcelain figures had captured the top end of the market, and pottery pieces were produced to a lower standard in order to achieve mass appeal.

Prattware
A large number of figures were produced by the Pratt family, and their distinctive form of lead-glazed earthenware, which was later copied by other local potters, became known as Prattware. The factory was founded c.1755 by William Pratt, and was taken over by his elder son Felix in 1810.
* Prattware is characterized by relief decoration in conjunction

with underglaze colours, mainly a brownish ochre, dull blue and green.

* The crude, daubed effect seen on the figure of a naval officer in the main picture, is typical of Prattware.
* As well as figures, the Pratts also made jugs and oval plaques.

Later 19thC figures

Figures made later in the 19thC were decorated with low-fired enamel colours, which created a wider and more subtle palette than their high-fired equivalent in the main picture. Note the pale-pink sash on this portrait bust of a poet or philosopher (c.1820), below.

* The features on this model are sharper and more clearly delineated, which may suggest a later production date.

Staffordshire groups such as this one featuring Romulus and Remus c.1820, and other classically inspired subjects, were very popular at the beginning of the 19thC. The bright, overglaze colours, particularly blue, superseded the duller Prattware tones.

* Notice the small impressed title at the base of the groups below left and below, another common feature at this time.

Modelled in the style of Obadiah Sherratt, who produced some of the most sought-after Staffordshire figures, this group "Tee Total" (c.1830), is an interesting hybrid. The thick foliage or bocage in the background, is a throwback to 18thC rococo figures. The medieval castle, reminds us that the gothic was enjoying a revival at this time.

* Pastel and primary colours are combined in a typical palette of the period.
* Models which have no moulding on the back are known as "flatbacks" and are highly collectable.

Subjects

A huge number of different figures and groups were made, including preachers, statesmen, politicians, military and naval leaders, sportsmen, actors, circus performers and criminals, as well as pastoral and romantic scenes.

Fakes and copies

These pieces have been extensively copied, faked and even reproduced using original moulds.

* Modern copies are often made by slip casting using a pale, chalk-like clay.
* It is important to be familiar with the range of colours used by the major manufacturers – going to auction viewings and museums, and using reference books can be very helpful.
* Later versions are nearly always lighter in weight than the originals.
* Be wary of pieces with a uniform network of cracks over the surface – this is not a feature of early 19thC Staffordshire pottery.

WEDGWOOD

A green and white jasper "Pegasus" vase, 19thC;
ht 20in (50.8cm); value code D

Identification checklist for Wedgwood's jasper ware
1. Does the piece have a smooth, silky surface?
2. Is the body colour pale cobalt blue, sage green, olive green, lilac, lavender or silky black (yellow is occasionally found)?
3. Is the body evenly stained and coloured throughout?
4. Does the surface feature white, low relief decoration?
5. Does the design depict a classical scene or motif?
6. Is the decoration crisp and finely executed?
7. Is there an impressed mark on the base?

Josiah Wedgwood (1730-95)
Trained as a potter from a young age, Josiah Wedgwood worked with a number of manufacturers before setting up his own business in Burslem in 1759.

During the early part of his career, Wedgwood made conventional Staffordshire-type pottery: tortoiseshell, agate, blackwares and moulded salt-glazed wares.

Creamware
From 1754 Wedgwood was closely involved with all the major developments in the production of earthenware and stoneware in Britain. The most notable of these was a cream-coloured clay body covered with a cream-coloured glaze. This "creamware" was widely copied throughout Europe.

This creamware coffee pot and cover made in the form of a cauliflower c.1765-80, is one of a series of wares made in this style by Wedgwood working, in association with the designer William Greatbatch.
* In 1765 Wedgwood was commissioned to produce a set of creamwares for Queen Charlotte, the wife of King George III. After this date, Wedgwood's creamware was renamed "Queen's Ware" in her honour.

Neo-classical influence
Wedgwood's partnership with Thomas Bentley led to the establishment of a new factory where they planned to produce vases and ornamental wares in the Classical style. It was called Etruria after a site in Ancient Greece where pottery had been excavated.

Black basaltes wares, such as this vase c.1775-80, were one form of Neo-classical stoneware produced at Etruria. Here Wedgwood has remained largely faithful to the vase's original form and decoration. These were almost certainly derived from archaeo-logical records compiled by Sir William Hamilton, a diplomat,

archaeologist and collector who had a great influence on neo-classicism in Britain.

Jasper ware
The vase in the main picture is a good example of Wedgwood's jasper ware, possibly the most distinctive of all his products.

Colours
Jasper ware was made in a range of colours: pale cobalt blue, sage green, olive green, lilac, lavender and silky black (yellow is rare).

Decoration
The crisp, white decoration, usually depicts classical scenes, that stand out in low relief (the decoration on fake jasper ware is less crisp, and tends to blur around the edges).

The effect on the surface of this vase c.1775-80 has been created using marbled slip rather than solid clay.
* Coloured slip was also used as a less expensive alternative when making later jasper wares after 1785, and was known as jasper dip.

Marks
Wedgwood was one of the first potteries to mark wares systemat-ically. Apart from the pre-Etruria wares which are very rarely marked, Wedgwood pieces are impressed with the full name, either of Wedgwood and Bentley, sometimes only the initials "WB" or Wedgwood alone. Invariably they are impressed, either in lowercase or in upper-case Roman letters. From 1860 a system of date coding using three letters was adopted.

MARTIN WARE

*A large Martin Brother's Bird, c.1898;
ht 13in (33cm); value code C/D*

Identification checklist for Martin Brother's birds
1. Does the bird have a detachable head?
2. Is the bird standing?
3. Are the feet and the beak finely and accurately modelled?
4. Does the bird's face have human characteristics?
5. Is the surface realistically textured?
6. Does the bird have a wooden base?
7. Is the glaze dimpled with an "orange peel" effect?
8. Is the piece fully signed and dated?
9. Is the mark incised (moulded marks are very rare)?

The Martin Brothers
Robert Wallace (b.1843), Charles Douglas (b.1846), Walter Frazer (b.1859) and Edwin Bruce (b.1860) Martin made distinctive stonewares at the end of the 19thC and the beginning of the 20thC. In 1877 they set up a pottery in Southall, Middlesex, and there the brothers worked as a team, designing, making and decorating their own pieces, in the spirit of the Arts and Crafts movement that developed in the second half of the 19thC. The Martin Brothers are often described as the first of the Studio potters.

Modelled wares
Robert Wallace, or Wallace, Martin had trained for a short time as a sculptor's assistant. He did some stone carving for the Houses of Parliament in London, and became interested in heraldic motifs and grotesque gargoyles. This fascination is clearly visible in the modelled wares produced by the Martin Brothers. These include birds (often resembling owls or parrots), such as the one in the main picture, and reptiles (mostly based on the toad). Often made with detachable heads, the models could be used as jars.

The bird in the main picture is very high quality and consequently is relatively expensive, but it does show all the characteristic features of this type of Martin ware:
* a face with human characteristics
* finely and accurately modelled feet and beak
* realistic surface decoration
* an "orange-peel" salt glaze in creams and browns
* a wooden base.

Wallace Martin also made a group of jugs and mugs decorated with grotesque faces, usually with flattened circular bodies, moulded with a face on each side.
* This piece was made c.1901; each side of the mug features a smiling face.

Thrown wares
The Martin Brothers also made a considerable number of other wares, including vases, jugs, punch bowls, whisky flasks, tobacco jars, oil lamp bodies, puzzle jugs, and even chamber pots.

Many pieces were decorated in a naturalistic style, as seen on this jug c.1894. The body has been incised with scrolling foliage in the type of design popularized by William Morris.

Other wares featured more realistic floral designs in a Japanese style, such as this vase c.1889. Edwin Martin prompted this change in style after producing a number of miniatures depicting canal-bank flowers or vegetation.
* Colours are subtle shades of green, blue, yellow brown and cream.
* Other decorative subjects include coiled dragons and lizards, birds and riverside subjects.
* Martin Brothers hollow wares are much less expensive than their models, and represent a good starting point for a collection of early Studio pottery.

The influence of the Art Nouveau movement around the turn of the century led to the production of a series of pots in organic shapes, such as gourds, pumpkins, marrows and other vegetables. The piece above, made c.1899, shows how the wares were incised with vertical and horizontal lines to give a realistic texture.

Marks
Pieces made by the Martin Brothers at Southall (1882-1914), are almost always incised "RW Martin & Brothers London & Southall", together with a number and a date.

WILLIAM DE MORGAN

A William De Morgan "Sunset and Moonlight Suite" charger
c.1900; dia. 18¼in (46.5cm); value code B/C

Identification checklist for De Morgan "Moonlight and Sunset Suite" lustre wares
1. Does the design feature birds, reptiles or dragons?
2. Is there also scrolling foliage?
3. Is the painting high quality?
4. Does the piece have a deep blue ground?
5. Does the surface feature a number of different-coloured lustres?
6. Is there a Morgan mark or an "FP" or "CP" monogram?
7. Has the design been documented?

William De Morgan (1839-1917)

After studying painting at the Royal Academy, De Morgan became interested in stained-glass design, and from 1863 he designed tiles and glass for the William Morris workshops. He began to decorate pottery with Islamic-style designs in 1869, and set up his own kiln. In 1873 he set up a workshop in Chelsea where he employed a group of assistants and a kiln operator. Later he hired two decorators, Fred and Charles Passenger.

De Morgan's premises moved a number of times, from Chelsea to Merton Abbey (1882), where he employed a thrower for the first time, and then to a fully-equipped factory in Sands End, Fulham (1888). These premises closed in 1907.

Tiles

De Morgan's early wares mainly comprised painted tiles for which he supplied the designs. Standard-sized tiles (6 x 6 in, 15 x 15cm), were bought in to the workshop as blanks and were then decorated.

"Persian" wares

One style of decoration favoured by De Morgan was called "Persian", although it is in fact based on Iznik wares made in Turkey in the 15thC.

This valuable vase has been decorated in the Iznik "Damascus" manner, with a characteristic palette that includes mushroom, sage-green, turquoise, purple, dark blue and black.
* Peacocks were a favourite De Morgan motif.
* The vase above was made at Merton Abbey and is stamped with an oval mark: "W De Morgan Merton Abbey".

Lustre wares

De Morgan was a great admirer of Islamic and Italian lustre wares, and after a great deal of experimentation was able to produce lustre colours using a variety of different metals. A range of coloured lustres were developed in the 1870s using copper and silver, including red, pink, yellow and soft-grey.

Possibly De Morgan's most distinctive lustre was ruby-red, seen here on this charger featuring a pair of lions.
* Pairs of animals, such as

antelopes, fish, and mythological beasts are a common motif.
* Ships are also a popular design.

An example of orange and yellow double lustre, this vase was made c.1890.

"Moonlight and Sunset" lustre

De Morgan considered his "Moonlight and Sunset Suite" triple lustre glazes on a deep blue ground, seen on the charger in the main picture, to be his finest achievement. Created using a combination of silver, copper, platinum and gold, they took him over 30 years to achieve.
* Although the piece in the main picture is of exceptional quality and therefore extremely valuable, other "Moonlight and Sunset Suite" wares can be bought for a tenth of the price, and smaller items, with less elaborate decoration, for even less.

Marks

De Morgan's mark is either impressed or painted on the base of his pieces.
* Some wares made at Merton Abbey feature a mark that includes an abbey together with "W De Merton Abbey".
* Other pieces are marked with a tulip.
* Wares made at the Sand's End factory feature marks such as a circular rose motif with "Wm De Morgan & Co Sands End Pottery Fulham" or a De Morgan stamp.
* Some wares feature the decorator's monogram, most commonly "FP" or "CP" (for Fred or Charles Passenger).

WILLIAM MOORCROFT

A Moorcroft-Macintyre "Florian" ware pedestal vase, c.1900;
ht 10in (25.4cm); value code F

Identification checklist for Moorcroft's "Florian" wares
1. Is the piece made from earthenware?
2. Has it been hand-made?
3. Is there a mark on the base?
4. Does the decoration comprise swirling, naturalistic motifs?
5. Is the design symmetrical?
6. Does the design cover the whole of the piece?
7. Has the decoration been tube-lined?

William Moorcroft
(1872-1945)
Staffordshire potter William
Moorcroft headed the Art Pottery
Department of Burslem-based
Macintyre & Co. (established
c.1847) from 1898.
* Moorcroft's most famous design
is "Florian" ware, such as the
vase in the main picture. These
are a distinctive group of wares
painted with floral motifs, foliage
and peacock feathers. The wares
were sold at Liberty's in London,
and Tiffany's in New York.
* Moorcroft also produced
"Florian" ware vases in a more
elongated form than the vase in

the main picture. The designs
on these pieces are usually
symmetrical, with naturalistic,
floral decoration.
* In 1913, with the backing of the
Liberty family, Moorcroft set up
his own factory in Burslem.

"Tube-line" decoration
This form of decoration, seen on
the vase in the main picture, is
another characteristic of Florian
ware. The technique involves
piping lines of slip onto the
surface of the piece and then
firing it. Glaze is then painted
between the lines. The overall
design then appears in low relief.

Marks

Moorcroft signed all Florian wares, usually with "W. MOORCROFT des." or just "WM des".

Sometimes pieces were marked "FLORIAN WARE JAS. MACINTYRE & CO. LTD BURSLEM ENGLAND", seen on the base of the vase in the main picture, shown above.
* After Moorcroft established his own factory W. Moorcroft (Ltd.), his pieces were marked "MOORCROFT BURSLEM".
* Moorcroft's signature mark was registered as a trade mark in 1919, but was previously used on some articles made while he was working at the Macintyre factory.

Other wares

After 1913 Moorcroft's range of wares expanded to include a number of different colourways and designs.
* Colours on his later wares are usually rich and bright, with a shiny glaze.

Moorcroft named the combination of rich glazes on this vase c.1939, "Flambé". This style developed into range that included a variety of wares featuring many different designs, such as Moorcroft's famous "Leaf and Berry", "Pansy", "Freesia", "Anamone", "Orchid", "Waratah" and "Toadstool" patterns.

Moorcroft's "Pansy" design which appears in a number of different colourways, is seen on this delicately-coloured vase c.1914.

Made in the "Pomegranate" pattern, this flared cylindrical vase was another form commonly used by Moorcroft.
* Note how the decoration extends over the rim of the piece, a feature found on a number of Moorcroft's wares.

Collecting

While some of Moorcroft's art pottery can be expensive, especially large and unusual items, his smaller wares featuring the same high quality painting and decoration, are more affordable.

CLARICE CLIFF

*A Clarice Cliff "crocus" teapot, c.1928;
ht 4½in (11.5cm); value code F/G*

Identification checklist for pottery designed by
Clarice Cliff
1. Does the piece have a mark on the base?
2. Is the form very modern?
3. Is the piece an item of tableware (decorative pieces
such as figures and masks are less common)?
4. Does the decoration comprise bold motifs?
5. Is the design hand-painted?
6. Are the colours bright and vivid?
7. Is there any black outline or banding around the
rims or motifs?
8. If the design features a landscape, is it very stylized?

Clarice Cliff (1899-1972)
A major figure in British pottery
in the 1920s and 30s, Clarice
Cliff joined A.J. Wilkinson's
Royal Staffordshire Pottery at
Burslem in 1916, where she was
taught modelling, firing, gilding
and pottery design. In 1927 Cliff's
talent and enthusiasm encouraged
her employers to provide her
with a studio, a small group of
assistants, and a brief to hand-
decorate 720 pieces of existing

whiteware. She used bold, geometric designs with vivid colours.

Marks
Most pieces by Clarice Cliff are
marked, often with impressed
dates (which may refer to the
date of manufacture, rather than
the year of decoration), and the
pattern name frequently appears
alongside Clarice Cliff's signature.
Pattern marks were initially
hand-written (before c.1931);

they were later stamped and eventually were lithographed.
* Fake marks are often crackled, although this effect occasionally appears on genuine pieces.

Some designs featured stylized landscapes, such as this "Orange Autumn" jug, c.1932. Landscapes also appear in other designs.

This jug is a typical example of the early abstract designs known as "Bizarre Ware" produced by Clarice Cliff in 1928. The bold, thickly applied, enamelled motifs are outlined in black, and the piece is covered with a honey-coloured glaze.

Wares
* The vast majority of Cliff wares are tablewares: jugs, teapots, coffee pots, cups, plates, toast racks, chargers, jam pots, sugar bowls, biscuit barrels and jardinières.
* Sets of tablewares were made in a variety of named styles, such as the "Athens" jug shown above, and the "Stamford" teapot in the main picture. "Conical", "Bonjour" and "Tankard" are other popular designs.
* Although more unusual, Cliff also made decorative pieces such as masks, plaques, figurines and candlesticks.

Decoration
After the initial "Bizarre Ware", Cliff's pottery featured designs with names such as "Crocus" (seen on the teapot in the main picture), "Melon", "Sungay", "Gayday" and "Berries".
* Designs appear in various colourways, and some are extremely rare.
* "Crocus" appears in many different colours, including Spring, Autumn, Blue, and Purple which is the most unusual.
* Some pieces feature experimental decorative techniques, such as the streaked "Delicia" design.

Fakes
Fakes of Clarice Cliff wares do exist, but usually exhibit the following features:
* a poor standard of painting with washed-out colours,
* a murky-coloured glaze that is unevenly-applied,
* a lack of overall definition, both in shape as well as decoration.

Style names
Not all the original names for Cliff's designs are generally known, and in many cases collectors have given names to certain designs until new discoveries are made and correct names can be attributed.

* Also known as "Bizarre Trees and House", this "Alpine" bowl was made in the early 1930s.

Collecting
* Common designs such as "Crocus" will be relatively inexpensive, but look out for unusual colourways.
* Pieces from the green, purple and black series known as "Inspiration", are highly sought after.

CARDEW &
STAITE MURRAY

*An earthenware charger by Michael Cardew;
dia. 14in (36cm); value code F*

Identification checklist for slipwares by Michael Cardew
1. Is the piece porous?
2. Do the colours include a rich chestnut-brown and a golden honey-yellow?
3. Is the surface covered with trailed slip or scratched decoration?
4. Is the glaze slightly crazed?

Michael Cardew (1901-82)

A key figure in 20thC British art pottery, who trained with Bernard Leach in the 1920s, Cardew left to start his own pottery in 1926 at Winchcombe, Gloucestershire. He made functional items in slip-decorated, lead-glazed earthenware, inspired by old English pottery traditions. In 1939 he established another pottery at Wenford Bridge, near Bodmin in Cornwall. Following a period in West Africa from 1942, Cardew began to produce brightly-glazed stonewares. From 1949 he travelled between Britain and Africa, researching, lecturing, writing and potting, and also went on a number of tours.

Glaze

Cardew's early slipwares are renowned for their lead glaze, which was made in the traditional way from led sulphide (galena), rather than the more reliable lead oxide glaze favoured by Bernard Leach at this time. Cardew's pots were glazed raw and once-fired, which gave erratic results, but when successful the colours are very impressive, a rich chestnut-brown and a honey yellow.
* The charger in the main picture, made at Winchcombe, is painted with white slip over the main surface, and decorated with wavy lines in brown slip. The lead-glazed colours are typically rich and strong.

Decorated with green slip, this cider jar has been scratched through with a characteristic pattern.
* Cardew's wares usually feature trailed or scratched designs that were spontaneous and original.
* A skilled pot thrower, Cardew's forms are generally bold and robust.

Porosity had been continuing problem for Cardew's earthenwares, and in the 1930s he sought to solved this by using a vitreous black glaze. He did not solve the problem, but the black glaze added to his decorative range.
* The characteristic design on the bowl above, is similar to a set of black-glazed plates that were intended to be sold at Heal's in London, c.1935.

Wares

Cardew produced a huge range of domestic items in slipware, including vases, jugs, cider bottles, bowls, plates, chargers, teapots and oil lamps.

Stonewares

Cardew spent long periods in Africa around Ghana and the countries of the Gold Coast. He produced some beautiful pieces of stoneware, glazed in dark green with vibrant red flashes of iron, and blue-grey.

William Staite Murray (1881-1962)

William Staite Murray is regarded by some as one of the main influences on 20thC ceramics. Murray set up his own pottery in 1919 at Rotherhithe in London, and inspired by Eastern philosophy, produced pieces that were almost all in the Oriental style. Like Cardew, Murray lived in Africa, although during his 22 years in Rhodesia (now Zimbabwe), he made no pots, and showed little interest in the local craft.
* Murray made simple pots and vases with monochrome glazes, and sometimes with splashed or brushed decoration.

Made c.1924, this vase is covered with a grey-green glaze, and has an incised mark on the base "W.S. Murray, 1924, London".
* The decoration on Murray's later wares became more sophisticated with high quality brushwork, and he also used a greater variety of techniques, including incised and inlaid decoration.
* Murray marked his early pieces using an incised mark, but after c.1924 he used an impressed "M" seal.
* Murray's wares are relatively inexpensive, and represent a good starting point for a collector of Studio pottery.

BERNARD LEACH &
SHOJI HAMADA

A stoneware vase by Bernard Leach decorated with leaping fish; ht 11¾in (30cm); value code E/F

Identification checklist for Bernard Leach

1. Has the pot been influenced by Oriental wares (although some pieces are based on medieval English pottery and slipware)?
2. Is the piece thickly-potted?
3. If there is any painted decoration is the brushwork very high quality?
4. Is the decoration simple, perhaps with some repetition?
5. Does the decoration comprise only one or two different colours?
6. Does the piece have a "BL" seal?

Bernard Leach (1887-1979)
Regarded by many as the founder of the 20thC Art Pottery movement, Leach originally trained in London as a graphic artist. On a visit to Japan in 1909 he became interested in Oriental ceramics, and learned the craft from some of the most experienced potters in Japan. Leach returned to England in 1920 and established a factory in St. Ives in Cornwall. As well as being a prolific and inspired craftsman,

Leach was also a talented artist, a successful author, and a respected teacher.

Influences
An interest in Eastern philosophy as well as a fascination with Oriental crafts were the guiding forces behind a large proportion of Leach's work.

The vase in the main picture and this slab bottle, c.1970 have a strong Oriental feel. Forms are bold, simple and functional.
* Later in his career Leach was also influenced by medieval English pottery and slipware.

Colour
* Leach did not use a wide variety of colour; most wares are brown, cream, grey, ochre, brownish-black, or combinations of these.
* The brownish-black glaze used on Leach's wares is known as *temmoku* and was originally used in China during the Song dynasty (960-1280). *Temmoku* wares were sought after by the Japanese who used them in the Tea Ceremony.

Decoration
* Many of Leach's wares feature painted decoration, such as the leaping salmon on the vase in the main picture. Other popular motifs were the wandering pilgrim, the flying bird and the running hare. The brushwork is of exceptionally high quality.
* Leach also experimented with a wide variety of other decorative techniques such as inlay, *sgraffiato*, wax resist, stencils, trailing, combing and fluting.

Shoji Hamada (1891-1978)
Having met Leach in Japan in 1918, Shoji Hamada accompanied him to England in 1920. He helped Leach establish the St.

Ives pottery, and produced enough pots for two London exhibitions before he returned to Japan in 1924. The quality of Hamada's work at St. Ives inspired many English potters to produce similar wares.

One of his most famous glazes, the *kaki* glaze on this hexagonal vase c.1958, was made from clay local to the pottery community where Hamada worked in Japan.
* Hamada's work is characterized by freedom and spontaneity; early wares are relatively subdued, but his later work included a greater variety of form and colour.

This angular stoneware vase with painted decoration c.1960, is a fine example of Hamada's work.
* Hamada's pottery reflected his belief in Zen philosophy, with its tenets of honesty, utility, humility and repetition.
* Decoration usually features brushed iron designs.
* Following his return to Japan in 1924, Hamada no longer signed his work. Those pots made at St. Ives were marked with the symbol *Sho*.

LUCIE RIE &
HANS COPER

A composite stoneware vase, c.1982;
ht 9½in (24.2cm); value code D/E

Identification checklist for stoneware by Dame Lucie Rie

1. Does the piece have a spontaneous, clearly hand-made look?
2. Does the glaze not quite reach the foot or base of the piece?
3. Is the foot well-finished?
4. Does the piece have a deep footring?
5. Is there an impressed "LR" seal on the base?
6. Is the glaze thick and pock-marked?
7. If the body of the piece has been embellished, is there *sgraffiato* decoration?

Lucie Rie (1902–1995)
Trained as a potter in Vienna where she was born, Lucie Rie came to England with her husband in 1938. Although he moved to the United States in 1939, Lucie remained in London during the war, where she set up her own studio and also produced buttons.

She met, and was influenced by, the major British Studio potters of the time, such as Bernard Leach and William Staite-Murray, but was able to develop her own, distinctive style. Rie continued to produce pots until her death in 1995, and is one of the world's most respected ceramic artists.

Forms
* Rie's work is characterized by simple, elegant forms which have a spontaneous, clearly hand-made look. Her flared, conical bowls, such as the one below, often appear slightly uneven.
* Another distinctive shape is illustrated by the piece in the main picture. This tall vase with a flared lip was made in more than one piece to simplify the process. Once dry the pot was sand-papered to smooth out the join.

Colours and glazes
Rie experimented widely with different coloured clays, glazes and their application.

Possibly Rie's most distinctive glaze was developed early in her career, and appears thick and pitted, as seen on this bowl c.1940.

As well as single-coloured glazes, Rie also worked with subtle, mottled colours heightened by the use of metal oxides, and sometimes combining different-coloured clays to create a swirled effect, such as on the "potato" pot below left, c.1982.

Decoration
* Additional decoration on Rie's wares was usually very simple, such as the bronze bands on the vase in the main picture.
* Rie's porcelain wares often feature *sgraffiato* decoration.

Hans Coper (1920-81)
Between 1946 and 1958 Rie shared a studio with Hans Coper, a refugee from Saxony. Employed as an assistant in her button factory, Coper showed such application that Rie introduced him to her potting techniques. Coper went on to become one of the most influential 20thC potters, but sadly he died in 1981.

This "thistle" form stoneware piece by Hans Coper c.1972, is a typical industrial-style design. The body is covered with a creamy, thick pitted glaze which is reminiscent of Rie, but the shape is entirely original. One of Coper's most famous forms is the spade, first exhibited in 1967.
* Hans Coper's pots are charac-terized by their idiosyncratic, machine-age forms, textured surfaces, and monochrome colour schemes.

Marks
* Pieces by Rie feature an impressed "LR" seal (approx. ½in, 1.5cm in length) made from plaster of Paris.
* Coper's mark is an impressed "HC" seal.

AMERICAN POTTERY

Rockingham glazed teapot, Baltimore, Maryland, c.1860-90

The decorative ceramics industry in North America has grown on a relatively small scale. The tradition of using mostly imported ceramics continues in the United States and Canada, where a significant proportion of useful and ornamental porcelain is of English, French or Japanese origin. Even inexpensive earthenware used in the clay-rich United States is often imported from Mexico, South America or Mediterranean Europe.

The relative lack of enterprise among American potters is a testament to the highly competitive standards, distribution systems and prices of imported ware in the two centuries since United States independence. It is also due in part to the tendency for early, colonial settlers to use imported ware, (some of which may have been among the possessions they carried to the "New World"), which was superior to any domestically-made wares, and familiar in form and style.

The early settlers of New England would have used mostly English or Dutch tin-glazed earthenware in their homes, much of which was carried on their journeys, with other prized possessions including pewter tableware. Small kilns were begun to meet the demands for inexpensive, useful items of crockery within the New England colonies. By the mid-17thC several settlements in Massachusetts, New York and Connecticut had potters, the first of whom was probably one Philip Drinker, active in Charlestown, Massachusetts by 1635. Little is known of these early endeavours, but output was probably extremely small and limited to crude, red earthenware with simple, lead glaze, in traditional north European forms. This early colonial style in pottery, characterized by simplicity and practicality, continued in popular production until the end of the 19thC. This can lead to some confusion with respect to dating, as items which appear to a European eye to be of 18thC origin or earlier may have been made for the rugged demands of a settler in the middle of the 19thC, or even later. This issue is further confused by the continued manufacture of this type of ware in some communities which have remained primitive and rural for puritanical religious reasons.

The cottage industry scale of domestic potting in North America lasted throughout the late 18th and early 19thC. Many potteries were established within brickworks and made little more than simple redware for local consumption. By the second half of the 18thC, a distinctively American style of slip-decorated redware was being made in several parts of New England, particularly Connecticut. This ware, much of which was actually made in Staffordshire for the American market, is commonly referred to as "slipware", or, somewhat erroneously, "Pennsylvania redware." The ware was made commercially until the early 20thC, and is now widely reproduced.

Another distinctively American style was developed in the manufacturing of salt-glazed stoneware. The simple, crude redware of local potters proved too fragile and porous for many needs, and a stoneware industry developed in colonial America on a more widespread scale. Most of the early efforts in stoneware production were by French and German immigrants, who made pale coloured, thickly potted crocks in several southern colonies, including Virginia and Georgia, as well as in New York and parts of New England, by the middle of the 18thC. Southern production proved more successful in the early stoneware period owing largely to the local availability of suitable fire clays, which were not abundant further north. Improved communications and greater affluence in the north east drew stoneware manufacturers to New England and as far north as Vermont after the war of Independence however, and the familiar style of blue-decorated "crocks" evolved. The 19thC also saw the development of a commercial potting industry in several parts of the United States beyond New England, where, with the exception of the Bennington works in Vermont, potting remained on a "cottage industry" scale. The new centres in Victorian America included several towns in Ohio and Pennsylvania, Baltimore in Maryland and Trenton, the state capitol of New Jersey, which was known as the "Staffordshire of America" by the 1880s. Utilitarian ware was made at all centres, but much of it was ornamental in keeping with modern taste.

In the late 19thC, an art pottery industry was established in North America, where works were established as far afield as New Orleans, California and New Hampshire. The best known, largest and most influential art pottery manufacturer was the Rookwood factory. Majolica ware, much of which was of distinctively American design and coloration, was also made by the 1880s, although on a smaller scale.

THE BENNINGTON
POTTERIES

Salt-glazed stoneware crock by E. and L.P. Norton, Bennington, Vermont, c.1861-81; ht 12in (30.5cm); value code F

Identification checklist for Bennington stoneware crocks

1. Is the body a pale buff colour, shading to pale grey?
2. Is the shape one of the two standard forms illustrated here (see main picture and above left on opposite page)?
3. Does the piece feature decoration in underglaze cobalt-blue (although yellow-ochre is occasionally found)?
4. Does the piece have an impressed mark including the name Bennington, or an address in Vermont (Vt.)?

Bennington

The town of Bennington in what is now the state of Vermont, was founded c.1749 by Benning Wentworth, the governor of New Hampshire under King George II. The tradition of potting in the town is largely the legacy of John Norton (1758-1828), who settled in the community as a farmer and distiller in 1785 and probably began a kiln in 1793.

The Norton Potteries (c.1793-1894)

The century of potting by the Norton family in Bennington was the largest stoneware-making enterprise in North America. The high standards achieved

and variety of successful forms set standards which were widely copied, particularly throughout New England, until the beginning of the 20thC when stoneware became virtually obsolete.

Decoration

The majority of Norton stoneware is plain, especially wares made pre-1830, but larger examples are often simply decorated. The embellishment gives a crock most of its collectable interest and value.
* Virtually all decoration is in underglaze cobalt-blue (although yellow-ochre was used at some periods).
* Typical images include stylized flowers (the least collectable),

insects, ornamental numerals, animals, birds, landscapes and commemorative images, which are among the most desirable.
* Some images are characteristic – for example, a butterfly is associated with the mid-1830s.

Made in Somerset, Massachusetts, this jug c.1850-80 and the crock in the main picture comprise the two standard forms of Bennington-type stoneware.
* Several modified forms were also produced, including barrel-shaped water coolers fitted with a bung near the base, covered pots for cream, milk and preserves, chamber pots, ink pots, spittoons, flower pots and jugs of various forms for milk or syrups, such as molasses.
* All Bennington stoneware is saltglazed, but some jugs and smaller items were coated in brown-tinted salt glaze. The wares are more thickly-potted and larger than items of European brown wares, and most forms are distinctly American.

Marks

A good deal of Norton stoneware is unmarked, particularly the smaller items. Marked crocks feature the name or initials of the potter, sometimes including the name Bennington and/or Vermont (Vt.), impressed and sometimes highlighted in blue. The stamped mark generally appears high on the wall of the vessel, above any decorative device. The name Norton may appear on stoneware made by family members operating in Connecticut. Crocks are sometimes stamped with the name and address of a retailer. A numeral or measure symbol often accompanies the mark. Unusual, early, marked wares are the most collectable.

Other Bennington potteries

Bennington was home to several potteries during the 19thC, most of which were engaged in the production of earthenware glazed in opaque, lustrous brown termed "Rockingham" ware. The best known and largest of these factories was the United States Pottery of Bennington, founded in the 1840s by Christopher Fenton and active throughout the 19thC.

Decorated with Rockingham glaze, this vase has been made in the form of a fireman's trumpet. Termed a "Bennington-type" piece, it was produced by one of the many smaller factories which copied the United States Potteries' styles and forms.
* These included a range of slip-cast hollow ware, notably jugs, with elaborate relief moulded decoration, all types of household items, figural flasks and statues.
* Most of the ornamental figural work in Rockingham glaze featured animals, particularly lions and dogs, modelled with crude but charming naiveté.
* The inspiration for a good deal of Bennington earthenware models came from Staffordshire, but the standards of execution typically inferior to English ware. Bennington pottery tends to be very thickly potted from a yellowish body. The scale of objects is generally noticeably larger than that of Staffordshire.

Marks

Very little Bennington pottery is marked, but impressed trade names or monograms may appear. It should also be noted that the ware is widely reproduced.

OTHER 19THC AMERICAN POTTERY

Lead-glazed redware ewer of early type, New England, c.1700-50; ht 10in (25.4cm); value code F

Identification checklist for 19thC American Pottery (not including Art Pottery)
1. Is the body thickly potted?
2. Is the object of a simple, utilitarian type associated with pre-industrial Europe?
3. Is any modelling or painted decoration relatively crude or naively applied?
4. If the decoration features a motif, is it uniquely or distinctively American?
5. Is the form derived from a European original?
6. Is the scale larger than comparable items of European origin?
7. Is there a mark of an American manufacturer or retailer?

Other 19thC American pottery
Domestic American Victorian pottery falls into six main categories: stoneware, redware, yellow ware, spatterware and spongeware, majolica, and native American wares.

Salt-glazed stoneware
Salt-glazed "Crocks" were manufactured on a widespread scale in the eastern United States during the 19thC (see pp. 154-5).

* This type of ware is classified as folk art and is very collectable. While rare pieces can fetch large sums, more ordinary 19thC wares are more readily affordable.

Redwares
Red-bodied earthenware, such as the piece in the main picture, is the earliest and most common American pottery. More collectable pieces are decorated with yellow slip using abstract, trailed

designs, mottos, or, rarely, pictures. Wares with unusual decoration, commemorative images, dates and marks (extremely rare), are particularly sought after.
* Typical wares include plates, pie dishes and deeper "pans".
* Value is determined largely by decoration and condition.

Yellow wares
Yellow earthenware of any body colour, including granite ware, can be termed yellow ware when covered with an opaque, yellow glaze.

Typical yellow wares are inexpensive, utilitarian bowls used for the preparation and storage of foods, such as this mixing bowl from Liverpool, Ohio, c. 1880.
* Yellow ware is very rarely marked and, although it is widely collected, examples are fairly common, typically plain and affordable.

Spatterware and Spongeware
These terms refer to a loosely-applied, random style of decoration, usually in cornflower blue or iron-red, over a grey or buff-coloured pottery body, under a clear, lead glaze.

Kitchen utensils, for preparation and serving, such as this sponge-ware pitcher, c.1900, are common and the technique was widely practised among North American potteries, especially during the last half of the 19thC.
* The most valuable examples

are those with painted polychrome decoration, often featuring a bird or landscape within a spattered or sponged border.
* Simple bowls or jugs are easily found and inexpensive.

American Majolica
American manufacturers began making majolica during the 1870s, and major centres include Baltimore, Maryland, East Liverpool, Ohio and Trenton, New Jersey.

The largest and best known manufacturer was Griffen, Smith and Hill of Phoenixville, Pennsylvania, who made the oyster plate shown above. Made with a trademark, "Etruscan Majolica" 1867-1902, these wares are very collectable today.
* Typical pieces, such as begonia leaf shape dishes, are common.
* A good deal of American majolica is signed, but it can also be identified by a thickly-potted body and crude decoration.

Native American Pottery
Perhaps the only pottery that can be regarded as unqiuely American is that made by the native people. The majority of American Indian pottery of 19thC origin was made in the south-west by tribes including the Hopi and Navajo, or in the extreme north-west. Most ware is black or red-bodied and all items are of traditional design and manufacture, which includes coil forming and, more commonly, wheel throwing. Decoration is typically geometric and stylized and rarely in polychrome.
* 19thC Native American pottery especially if made before the centennial of 1876, is rare and highly sought after.
* More recent examples of traditional-style wares are common, and many will be marked.

ROOKWOOD

A Standard Glaze vase decorated by Matthew Daly for Rookwood, c.1886; ht 44½in (113cm); value code C/D

Identification checklist for Rookwood Standard Glaze wares
1. Is the piece made from earthenware?
2. Is it heavily potted?
3. Has it been slip cast?
4. Does the decoration comprise coloured slips applied under a clear, high glaze?
5. Does the ground colour blend from one tone to another?
6. Does the design include flowers, animals, landscapes, or portraits of Native Americans?
7. Is the piece marked with an impressed signature, date, code letters and an artist's monogram?

Rookwood (1880-1941)

Founded in Cincinnati by Maria Longworth Nichols, the Rookwood pottery was named after the home of her father, 19thC arts patron Joseph Longworth. Influenced by the style and quality of Japanese ceramics, the company set out to produce Art Pottery with naturalistic decoration to a high standard.

Early wares

In the early years Rookwood produced mainly heavily-potted, slip-cast or thrown wares in dark colours. Many were made in Japanese forms, and painted with floral motifs. Already a success in the United States, the Paris Exposition of 1900 brought Rookwood to the attention of the European market.

Decoration

Frequently influenced by Art Nouveau, decorative motifs used at Rookwood include indigenous American flora.
* The sunflowers on the vase in the main picture were a popular Art Nouveau motif.

Made in 1890, this bowl is painted with sprays of flowers in a typical palette.
* Other motifs include Oriental-style flowers and dragons.
* A group of wares were made painted with portraits of Native Americans; those decorated between 1897 and 1903 by William P. McDonald and Matthew A. Daly (who painted the vase in the main picture), are the most collectable.

"Standard" glazes

In 1883 the Rookwood slip-painting technique was refined to make the glaze more even, and to give greater colour contrasts. The result, known as "Standard glaze" gave the ground a graduated effect, moving from one tone to another. The glaze is clear and bright.
* The variation of colour over the piece is clearly seen on the vase in the main picture.

Several versions of the Standard glaze were developed at Rookwood. Colours include "Sea Green", a pale green, "Iris" a pale, muted grey, and a mottled effect known as "Goldstone" or "Tiger-eye".

* A rare piece, the "Iris" glaze vase above with a black background, was made around 1900 by John Hamilton Delany Wareham.

Vellum glaze

In 1904 Rookwood patented a matt glaze called "Vellum", which became the major form of decoration on their wares after 1901.
* Vellum-glazed wares usually feature stylized flowers, such as wisteria, crocus and orchid, forest scenes or sailing boats.

Made in 1923, this vellum vase with a blue ground, is decorated with trees and marshland.

GEORGE E. OHR

Bulbous-bottomed vase with cylindrical neck and two kinked handles; ht 6½in (16.5cm); value code F

Identification checklist for pottery by George E. Ohr
1. Is the piece made from red earthenware?
2. Does it look obviously hand made, with the appearance of early Studio Pottery?
3. Is the piece thinly potted, with a lightweight, brittle feel?
4. Does the piece have an unusual, probably asymmetric, form?
5. Are the walls or rims crimpled or folded?
6. If the piece has handles are they thin and tendril-like?
7. If glazed, is the surface mottled and lustrous with a deep colour?

George E. Ohr (1857-1918)
An unusual character and virtuoso art potter, although never a commercial success, George E. Ohr opened a simple studio in the artist's colony of Biloxi, Mississippi in 1885. He worked alone apart from a brief association with the Newcomb College Pottery in New Orleans in the mid-1890s. His eccentric lifestyle and appearance (wide staring eyes and long moustaches) earned him the nickname "the mad potter of Biloxi". Most Ohr ware available to collectors comes from his personal collection (over 6,000 pieces that he could not bear to sell individually during his lifetime), made over as a legacy to his children, and recovered from storage in 1972.

Technique

Ohr used a wheel and a wood burning kiln, and produced hand-thrown wares which have the appearance of early Studio pottery. He worked almost exclusively in red earthenware, and pieces tend to be thinly-potted, with a lightweight, brittle, body as seen on the piece in the main picture.

Decoration

While many of Ohr's pieces were relatively plain, he also made wares with applied decoration, particularly tendril-like handles as seen on the vase in the main picture.

* Pieces with applied decoration often fetch higher prices, because they tend to be larger and more complex.

One of Ohr's favourite decorative techniques was to pinch, fold and press vessels, or parts of vessels into unusual shapes. This dimpled and folded vase is a good example of this technique, as is the bisque-fired pot below.

Bisque-fired wares

A large proportion of Ohr's wares were once-fired and unglazed, and are known as bisque wares.

The vase, below left, is a typical bisque ware piece, but Ohr also produced variations using coloured muds, clays marbled together, and some pieces were brushed with mineral pigment.

Glazes

Ohr's glazes are usually lustrous, mottled, and comprise the tones of green and brown that are easily achieved in a wood-burning kiln.

Made with a stove-pipe neck (a relatively common feature), this vase is a good example of the rich, mottled effect found on many of Ohr's wares.

* Other colours are also found, including blue (seen in the main picture), bronze, black, salmon and orange.
* Sometimes the colours are dappled over the surface of the piece giving a striking effect.

Marks and copies

* Most of George Ohr's pottery is signed, and usually impressed "G E OHR Biloxi Miss"; later examples bear an incised facsimile script signature.
* The wares are simple to copy, and their popularity has led to a number of forgeries that include convincing marks and can be difficult to distinguish from the originals.
* Copies are generally small with a red body and a mirror-black lustrous glaze.

FAKES & MARKS: ITALY

FAKES

From its earliest days of manufacture, maiolica has been eagerly collected; pieces were known as "Raphael" wares after the painter. As a result, fakes and forgeries exist in huge quantities, especially from the second half of the 19thC, and factories flourished by making copies of earlier masterpieces.

In the 19thC, the Florentine potter Ginori (see mark on facing page) was especially prolific in making copies of Faenza, Deruta and Castel Durante. This activity coincided with the *Historismus* movement in northern Europe, when German stoneware and lead-glazed Palissy wares were also reproduced. Even provincial pottery such as Sicilian wares are faked. For example, fakes of Caltagirone pottery were produced in the latter 19thC. They are weak, and their bases do not resemble condensed milk (see below).

Apart from factory-type production, the most skilled forgeries were made by Feruccio Mengaroni. His forgeries of classic maiolica are among his most accomplished pieces. The circular plaque above, was made c.1900-25. His wares have fooled experts in both Europe and the United States; a number of pieces have only recently been attributed to him.
* Mengaroni specialized in wares from Luca Della Robbia, Caffaggiolo and Faenza.
* To distinguish a fake, look at the margins of the piece where the treatment is likely to be weak and casual, rather than lively and original.

Bases

On Castel Durante and Urbino wares, look at the reverse of the piece. The glaze should be uneven and bubbled, with areas of pooling in turquoise patches. The rim and footrim should always be naturally worn.

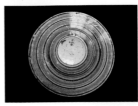

The reverse of this Faenza dish c.1520-25, shows the natural wear on the edge of the recessed base, the pinhole flaws in the glaze, and the potting blemishes found on most early pieces.
* The footrim is discoloured where it has absorbed dirt.

The footrim of this fake piece has been artificially worn in a circular motion, there is no discolouration. In addition, there are no pinholes in the white base, and relatively few imperfections on the sloping walls which are covered in a very smooth glaze.
* With careful scrutiny, diagonal scratch marks are visible on the outer ochre band, which would not occur on a naturally-worn piece.
* Note how the reflection of the window on the piece in this photograph is regular, while on the original it is not.

Borders

In order to make a piece appear as important as possible, fakers of maiolica often try to make the borders of their pieces extremely complex.

While the figures are generally good on this border from a fake piece, it features bright colours (particularly blue and green) which would not have appeared on an original. There is also too much space between the edge of the central design and the border.

This border illustrates the lively, fluent, confident designs found on genuine maiolica. The scale is correct and there is no unnecessary space between the centre and the rest of the design.

Ulysse Cantagalli (d.1901)
From 1878, Cantagalli made reproductions of early Urbino, Faenza, Gubbio, Deruta and della Robbia.

The Cantagalli mark was a cockerel that appeared in various forms.
* The unusual mark above, found on the base of a reproduction of an Urbino piece c.1880, is a partially-complete stencilled version.

MARKS
A great deal of work remains to be done in the study of marks found on Italian maiolica. Most of those found are based on stencil-type outlines which tend to obscure an artist's individuality.

The marks shown here, represent a selection of those found on Italian maiolica.

Caffaggiolo (nr. Florence)
Maiolica early 16thC–mid-18thC, marks include:

Castel Durante
Maiolica 16thC, marks include:

Doccia (nr. Florence)
Ginori 19thC, "GI", "GIN" and impressed "Ginori" found, also:

Faenza
Maiolica 14thC–16thC. Probably the mark of Maestro Virgiliotto Calamelli (died c.1570):

Gubbio
Maolica, especially known for ruby lustre wares, factory marks of Maestro Giorgio include:

Savona (nr. Genoa)
Mark of the Levantino family of Albissola:

Urbino
Marks of Francesco Xanto Avelli of Rovigo include:

FAKES & MARKS: FRANCE

FAKES

Fakers of French material concentrate on the later wares of Rouen, Strasbourg, Moustiers and Marseilles. These were manufactured in the latter half of the 19thC.

Forgers are especially interested in Rouen, Chinoiserie, *grand-feu* wares featuring the *à la Corne* pattern – a bold, swirling design. Forgeries are painted in a rather stiff manner, and the blue that is used is strong and bright, in contrast to the greyer blue used 1700-40.

The wares of Moustiers also attract attention, especially wares painted with grotesque dwarves and fantastic creatures, but these lack fluency. Many fakes feature full marks, but the handwriting is stilted.

Petit-feu wares from the Strasbourg and Marseilles factories are also copied. Veuve Perrin (Marseilles) pieces are extensively copied, usually wares featuring Chinoiserie or over-delicate rococo scenes (figures and landscapes), but over-fussy outlines give them away. The "VP" mark is one of the most common faience forgeries in Europe, so great care must be taken. If in doubt always seek the advice of an expert.

Samson of Paris imitated all "classic" 18thC faience manufacturers, including Strasbourg. But the material he used is the same for all the factories that he copied, and is easy to distinguish. Also, there is no undulating glaze, and no waxy softness characteristic of Strasbourg. He had his own mark, an intertwined "S" that appeared on the base of his pieces. It is possible to erase the mark, and this has occurred, but where it has been removed, abrasion marks are visible on the underside of the piece.

MARKS

A selection of marks found on French pottery are shown below.

Aprey (Haute-Marne)

Faience c.1744-c.1860. Founded by Lallemant, Jacques, Baron d'Aprey and Joseph Lallemant de Villehaut. Factory mark:

Lille

Faience 1696-1802:

Mark commonly found on modern forgeries:

Marseilles (Bouches-du-Rhône)

Faience 17th-19thC. Clérissy, Joseph (d.1685). Factory active until c.1743:

Fauchier factory 1711-c.1794:

Veuve Perrin factory c.1740-c.1795:

Robert's factory c.1750-c.1793:

Bonnefoy's factory 1762-c.1827 (Hard-paste porcelain also made from 1803.) Mark of Antoine Bonnefoy, artist (d.1793):

Moustiers (Basses-Alpes)
Faience 1679-19thC.
Olerys, Joseph, and Laugier, Jean
Baptiste 1738-c.1790:

Joseph Fouque (d.1800).
Jean-François Pelloquin 1749-
1852:

Faience tablewares, dinner
services and altar vases:

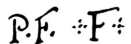

Nevers (Nièvre)
Faience 16th-19thC.
Mark on a group attributed to
Denis Lefebvre c.1629-49:

Niderviller
Faience from 1754.
Baron Jean-Louis de Beyerlé
1754-70.
Marks on faience:

Comte de Custine 1770-93:

Rouen (Seine-Infériure)
Faience from c.1526-19thC.
Late 17thC painters' marks
found on faience:

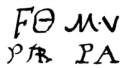

Guillibaud factory c.1720-50:

Pierre Heuge and family 1690-
early 19thC:

Paul Caussy, son and grandson,
1707-:

Saint-Amand-les-Eaux (Nord)
Faience, white and creamwares
1718-1818:

Sceaux
Faience c.1748-19thC
De Bey & Jacques
Chapelle:

Mark on faience:

Strasbourg (Alsace)
Faience.
Hannong factory 1721-81.
Faience marks of Paul Hannong
(c.1740-60):

Mark of Joseph Hannong
1762-81 (numerals refer to
pattern numbers, with many
numbers found):

FAKES & MARKS: HOLLAND

FAKES

Most forgeries of Dutch pottery, particularly Delft, were made in the late 19th and early 20thC, and are based on late 17th and early 18thC blue and white, and polychrome wares.

Among the more commonly faked pieces are wares by Adriaenus Koeks and his son Pieter Adriaenus Koeks. Their "AK" and "PAK" devices (see facing page and below) were used extensively by forgers and pieces with these marks should be examined with great care, perhaps by an expert.

Faked marks, such as the one above, exhibit a lack of cohesion and fluency. On this example, the pattern numbers appear to have been added as an afterthought.

Fakes of blue and white wares are inevitably fussily-painted with thin, spidery details, and figures have modern-looking faces. The man in the design above, has a beard which would never appear on genuine Delft wares.
* While the basic material is similar to earlier wares, the colour of the cobalt is brighter than the greyish tones of the originals.
* It is important to look for natural wear on the piece. There will be a breakdown of the glaze on the surface of the piece where it would have been handled, and also on the footrim.

Fakes tend to be made of more decorative pieces – for example, figures, vases and bottles, such as this one.
* The proportions of fakes are often wrong, such as the thin neck on this bottle. Here the overall shape is weak, and the decoration is stiff.

In 18thC Holland there was a huge industry for enhancing plain and blue and white wares with other colours, predominantly a distinctive blood red.
* The red found on genuine, Delft, Imari-style wares, features a much softer red.
* Known as "clobbering", these over-painted wares were not intended to deceive, and are usually painted in the Chinese or Japanese style, but there is a chance they could be mistaken for 18thC English polychrome delftwares, which are much more valuable.

MARKS

This list represents a selection of marks belonging to different factories, found on pottery made in the town of Delft, near Rotterdam in Holland.

De vergulde Blompot
("The Golden Flowerpot") Estd. 1654:

Het Bijltje
("The Hatchet") 1657-1802, mark registered in 1764 by Justus Brouwer:

Mark registered in 1680 by Quirinus Cleynoven, potter at *De porceleyne Fles, De Grieksche A.*

De porceleyne Fles
("The Porcelain Bottle") Estd. 1655:

Mark registered in 1764 by Johann and Dirk Harlees c.1795-1800:

Modern mark:

De Griecksche A
("The Greek A") Mark of Samuel van Eenhorn:

Adriaenus Koeks 1687-1701:

Adriaenus Koeks, his son Pieter and his widow:

De porceleyne Klaeuw
("The Porcelain Claw") Estd. 1760; one of a number of marks registered in 1764:

De 3 Klokken
("The Three Bells") Estd. 1671:

De Lampetkan
("The Ewer") Estd. 1637:

't Oude Moriaenshooft
("The Old Moor's Head) Estd. c.1690:

De Paauw
("The Peacock") Estd. 1652:

De metale Pot
("The Metale Pot") Estd. 1638; mark of Lambertus Cleffius 1666-1691 (also of "The White Star"):

De Roos
("The Rose") Estd. 1662:

Rous.

De dobbelde Schenckan
("The Double Tankard") Estd. 1659:

VE
IL
DS

De porceleyn Schotel
("The Porcelain Dish") Estd. 1612:

FAKES & MARKS: GERMANY

FAKES

Stoneware

Apart from the German potteries that have remained in continuous production, there have also been revivals of particular styles – for example, during the *Historismus* period in the late 19thC.

The white-bodied hollow wares of Siegburg were copied by Fleischmann and other factories, but these versions appear over-mechanical, and the forms are often wrong.

In addition, the base of original stonewares is gently concave, while copies are flat, and feature unconvincing thumb prints, as seen on the piece above, which has parallel, rather than rounded striations. On original stonewares, the potter would remove the piece from the wheel using a cheese wire that was dragged in a circular motion. (See pp.106-7 for a genuine example.)

Raeren wares were copied at the end of the 19thC. Originals have a machine-made look, but copies such as the one above, are very mechanical with precise stamping, turning, and neat bases. However, this piece can be identified as a copy by its mark; it is impressed with the initials "HS", that belong to the maker Hubert Schiffer, who was active in the Rhineland from 1880.

Westerwald wares have been made up to the present day, but later pieces can be identified by their precise turning and neat foot.

Faience

Relatively few fakes of German faience have been discovered.

MARKS

This list represents a selection of marks found on pottery made in Germany, organized by town.

Ansbach (Bavaria)

From c.1710.
Faience, white and cream-coloured earthenware.
Rare factory mark:

Popp, Johann, Georg Christoph 1715- (d.1786)
Marks include:

·Pop:

Bayreuth (Bavaria)

Faience c.1713-

Bayreu:

Knöller, proprietor 1728-44

BK ·B·X·

Pfeiffer, Johann Georg, proprietor 1760-67

B ·P·

Berlin (Prussia)
Faience and red earthenware
1678-18thC.
Funcke, Cornelius 1699-

Brunswick
Faience 1707-1807. Horn, Heinrich Christoph von Hantelmann, Werner von 1710-49:

Reichard, Johann Heinrich
Behling, Johann Erich 1749-56:

Cassel (Hesse-Naussau)
Faience 1680-1788.
Possibly mark of Johann Heinrich
Koch 1719-24:

Coburg (Thuringia)
Faience 1738-86:

Crailsheim (Würtemberg)
Faience c.1745-19thC:

Damm (nr.Aschaffenburg)
Cream-coloured earthenware
1827:

Dorotheenthal (nr. Arnstadt, Thuringia)
Faience c.1716-c.1806:

Eckernförde (Schleswig)
Faience 1765-85:

Probably the initials of Abraham
Leihamer painter, 1764-68:

Flörsheim (nr. Frankurt-am-Main)
Faience 1765-present:

Frankurt-am-Main
Faience 1666-c.1772:

Mark found on blue and white
Chinese-style wares:

Freiberg (Saxony)
Late 17thC stoneware, impressed
marks:

Fulda (Hesse)
Faience 1741-58
Arms of Fulda and signature of
Adam Friedrich von Löwenfinck:

Usual factory mark "FD" in
script.

Göggingen (nr. Augsburg)
Faience 1748-52:

Usual factory mark:

Hamburg
Faience c.1625.
Painters' marks include:

Hanau (Frankfurt-am-Main)
Faience 1661-1806:

1797-1806 cream-coloured
earthenware:

Hieronymus von Alphen period
1740-86.
Marks included:

Höchst (nr. Mayence)
Faience 1746-58.
Founded by Adam Friedrich von
Löwenfinck:

Kellinghüsen (Holstein)
Faience 18thC-

Kelsterbach (Hesse Darmstadt)
Faience and cream-coloured
earthenware.
Early faience mark:

Kiel (Holstein)
Faience 1763-88.
Many painters' marks, including

Tännich and Christopherson:

Künersberg (nr. Memmingen)
Faience 1745-c.1790:

Ludwigsburg (Wurtemberg)
Faience 1757-1824:

Magdeburg (Hanover)
Faience 1754-86.
Guichard, Johann Philipp:

Also "M Guischard" impressed
on cream-coloured earthenware
1786-1839.

Mosbach (Baden)
Faience and cream-coloured
earthenware 1770-.
"Carl Theodor", also claimed as
Frankenthal:

Also impressed "M" found on
cream-coloured earthenware after
1818.

Münden (Hanover)
Faience and glazed earthenware
1737-1854.
Mark of von Hanstein:

Nuremberg (Bavaria)
Faience 1712-c.1840.
Factory mark after 175:

Painter's marks including:

Probably Johann Rossbach painter, c.1715-:

Kordenbusch, Andreas, painter c.1726-(d.1754):

Marks of painter Georg Kordenbusch (d.1763) and his pupils included:

Offenbach (nr. Frankfurt-am-Main)
Faience 1739-early 19thC:

Osnabrück (Hanover)
Faience 1727-31:

Proskau
Faience 1763-93, earthenware to 1850.
Count Leopold von Proskau 1763-69:

"Dietrichstein" period:

"Leopold" period:

Raeren (nr Aix-la-Chapelle, Rhineland)
Stoneware c.1565.
Marks include incised initials and some dates.

Mark of Jan Emens c.1566-94:

Schleswig
Faience 1755-1814.
Probably Abraham Leihamer, painter c.1758:

Stockelsdorf (nr.Lübeck)
Faience 1771-19thC.
"Stockelsdorff-Buchwald-Abraham Leihamer" modeller and painter 1772-74, often with initials of painters:

Stralsund (Pomerania)
Faience c.1755-92.
Johann Eberhardt, Ludwig Ehrenreich c.1766:

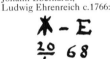

Wiesbaden (Nassau)
Faience and cream-coloured earthenware 1770-95.
"Wiesbaden-Dreste":

Erlemann, Fr. 1893-, earthenware:

Wrisbergholzen (Hanover)
Faience 1735-1834.
Factory mark:

Zerbst (Anhalt)
Faience 1720-68, 1793-1861.
Factory mark:

FAKES & MARKS: BRITAIN & IRELAND

FAKES

English delftware

There are fakes of 17thC wares, especially wine bottles. Many original wine bottles featured no marks or inscriptions; since ones with marks are the most sought after, fakers have added inscriptions to genuine pieces and refired them. This is indicated by blistering on the surface. Original 17thC handwriting is difficult to forge convincingly.

* White pieces are now often worth more than inscribed pieces because so few are available on the market.

* 18thC delftware has not been faked so extensively, because it is not as collectable as the earlier wares.

Slipware

Some very good forgeries of low-fired redware have been made. These are difficult to identify because the material has remained unchanged, and the decoration is primitive an relatively straightforward to reproduce. But in general, the designs on faked pieces are stiffer than on the originals.

In the past few years there has been controversy over the attribution of a group of owl jugs. Tested inconclusively by the Department of Archaeometry in Oxford, they were probably made in the 19thC.

*It is important to look for wear which should be natural.

Wedgwood

Attempts were made to copy Wedgwood's early cauliflower wares in the 1920s and 30s, but the colours are difficult to recreate (on later pieces the colours are harsh), and the moulding does not have the same detail or clarity.

An imitation of Wedgwood's "Cauliflower" ware, the teapot below left and above, can be identified as a fake by the fact that the drainage holes have been glazed over, showing that the piece could not be used for its intended function.

Wedgwood's later wares have been imitated both in Britain and on the Continent (even Sèvres copied his style). His work is rarely unmarked and there are few marked fakes. The control over the quality of Wedgwood's wares means that copies are less well-finished and generally lower quality.

* Note: there is a group of wares with the mark "Wedgwood & Co.", but this is a separate company. If you are aware of the correct marks that appear on Josiah Wedgwood's wares then you won't be deceived.

Salt-glazed stonewares

Copies of Astbury-type pew groups appeared in Britain in the 1920s, some with names of different potters, but clearly by the same hand. The original salt and lead-glazed figures made in primitive forms are relatively simple to reproduce convincingly. But, on the later versions, the modelling of the eyes, hands and knees is less defined. In addition, the originals have no marks.

Agateware cats have also been copied. Remember, the colours on the body should be clear, not muddy, and the modelling should be careful and sensitive.

Staffordshire figures

Flatbacks and cottages were extensively copied in the late 19th and early 20thC, and even today. These are poorly coloured, with insensitive detailing, and are generally unconvincing.

MARKS
This list represents a selection of marks found on pottery made in Great Britain and Ireland, organized by town.

England
Bristol
Delftware from c.1650:

Initials of Michael Edkins delft painter and his wife on plate dated 1760:

Chelsea (London)
Vyse, Charles, Studio potter 1919-c.1963.
Initials and also painted mark with year date added:

Clevedon (Avon)
Elton, Sir Edmund, Sunflower Pottery 1879-1930.
Mark 1879-1920:

Elton

Clifton Junction (nr. Manchester)
Pilkington Tile & Pottery Co. Ltd., earthenware and tiles 1897-1938, 1948-57.
Factory mark, Roman numeral here stands for 1908:

VIII

Designers also had their own marks.

Fulham (London)
De Morgan, William c.1872-1907, decorator of earthenwares
Impressed mark "W De Morgan" 1882-, "Co." added after 1888 marks used at Merton Abbey 1882-88 included:

Sand's End Pottery 1888-97, marks included:

Lambeth (London)
Doulton & Watts.
Stoneware, earthenware and salt-glazed wares, c.1815-58:

Doulton & Co. Lambeth c.1858-1956, Burslem (Staffordshire) 1882-.
c.1869-77, mark on decorated coloured wares. After 1872, year often appears in the centre:

Mark on decorated salt glaze, "England" added after 1891:

Burslem factory marks c.1882-1902 include:

London
Studio potters include:

Dalton, William B.
Stoneware and porcelain, Studio potter 1900-c.1955 (in United States from 1941).
Incised or painted mark:

WB

Martin Bros.
Stoneware, Studio potters 1873-1914.
Mark from 1882:

Murray, William Staite
Studio potter 1919-62 (in
Rhodesia from 1940).
Mark "WS Murray London" with
date.

Rie, Lucie
Studio potter, c.1938-present.
Impressed mark:

Poole (Dorset)
Cater & Co.
Earthenware 1873-1921.
Pieces marked "Carter & Co",
"Carter Poole".

Carter Stabler & Adams
1921-present, marked "Poole
England"; "Ltd. added 1925.
Mark from 1956:

Mark 1963-, "Poole Pottery Ltd."

St.Ives (Cornwall)
Leach, Bernard, 1921-79.
Leach Pottery marks:

Personal marks of Bernard Leach
(1889-1979):

Hamada, Shoji:

Staffordshire
Since the 17thC Staffordshire has
been the main pottery-producing
area in England. Types of pottery
produced include earthenware,
salt-glazed stoneware, jasper
ware, and later pottery bodies
developed after c.1880. Many different towns grew up around the
industry, including Burslem,
Cobridge, Hanley, Shelton and
Tunstall. As a rough dating guide,
the word "England" in the mark
dates a piece to 1891 or after.
This was required by the

American McKinley Tarriff Act
which demanded that the country
of origin be marked on pottery
exported to the United States.
"Made in England" suggests a
date of c.1920 onwards.
    Pottery was produced by such
a large number of manufacturers
in Staffordshire, that those shown
below represent only a small
selection.

Astbury (Shelton) mid-18thC
Earthenware, incised or
impressed "Astbury".

Carlton Ware Ltd.
Earthenware 1958- (Arthur
Wood & Son Group).
Modern printed mark:

Cooper & Co. J.
Earthenware, 1922-5, became
Susie Cooper Pottery (Ltd. from
c.1961).
Marks include:

Printed mark, 1932-:

Copeland & Garrett.
1833-present.
Mark on earthenware 1850-67:

Hall, Ralph
Earthenware 1822-49, printed in
backstamp "R. Hall", "& Son"
c.1836, "& Co. " after 1849.

Jones (Longton) Ltd., A. E.
Earthenware 1905-46
Printed or impressed mark:

PALISSY

Other "Palissy" mark continued
by Palissy Pottery Ltd., now a
subsidiary of Royal Worcester

Ltd. Not to be confused with
16thC French lead-glazed wares
by Bernard Palissy.

Moorcroft Ltd., W.
Earthenware 1913-, marked
"Moorcroft Burslem".
Signature of William Moorcroft
(d.1945):

Mark of son Walter:

Mountford, A .J.
Earthenware, 1897-1901. Many
marks on Staffordshire pottery
feature a knotted rope in varying
styles, with initials corresponding
to the manufacter:

BURSLEM

Neale & Co., James
All types of wares in the style of
Wedgwood c.1776-86, marked
"N", "Nealé", "I. Neale,
Hanley", "& Co." added c.1778.
Neale worked with many other
partners until 1795.

Newport Pottery Co. Ltd.
Earthenware 1920-, fully named
marks. Mark c.1938-66 "Clarice
Cliff" in script.

Wedgwood & Co.
Enoch Wedgwood (Tunstall), not
to be confused with Josiah
Wedgwood.

Wedgwood & Sons Ltd.
Josiah, rare incised initials "JW"
or signature c.1760-70:

Wedgwood & Bentley
partnership 1769-80, manufacture
of Neo-classical wares only,
marked "Wedgwood & Bentley",
sometimes with "Etruria",
impressed or raised mark on

cameos c.1780-98 "W. &. B":

From 1860 the Wedgwood factory
began to use a date-marking system as well as their name mark.
Comprising three letters, the first
indicated the month, the second
a potter's mark, and the third the
year of manufacture. These were
used cyclically. The system was
altered slightly in 1907 and 1930.

Winkle & Co., F.
Earthenware 1890-1931
misleading mark used 1908-25,
suggesting they were made by
18thC potter Thomas Whieldon
who did not mark his wares:

Wood, Ralph (1715-72), his son
(1748-95), and grandson (1781-
1801), marks include "R, Wood",
"Ra. Wood", sometimes with
"Burslem".

Welwyn Garden City
Coper, Hans 1947-
Studio potter:

Winchcombe (Gloucestershire)
Cardew, Michael A., Studio
potter c.1926-39, also at
Wenford Bridge c.1939-42
Impressed mark:

Wrotham (Kent)
Greene, John
Slipware potter c.1760,
slip-trailed mark "IG".

Ifield, Thomas, Henry and John
Slipware potters, slip-trailed
initials found on wares c.1620-75:
"TI", "HI", "II".

Ireland
Dublin
Delamain, Captain Henry
(d.1757)
Mark "HD" in monogram, and
also this mark 1752-c.1771:

Dublin

FAKES & MARKS: OTHER CENTRES

CHINA
Fakes
With the discovery of Tang tombs in the early 20thC, pottery began to flood to the West and created some interest among fakers. In the 1920s a number of unglazed and strawglazed figures appeared on the market. But the fakes are clumsily potted in the wrong material with a lack of detail, and are therefore easy to distinguish. In the post-War period there was an increase in the numbers of tourists to China and Hong Kong and the market became saturated, especially in the more sculptural types of Tang, such as camels and especially horses.

Other fakes are more sophisticated. In the past 20 years Song wares have appeared, including Japanese and Chinese copies of Lonquan celadons and *temmoku* teabowls from Fujian. The latter are the most convincing, but are usually mechanical in form, and lacking in characteristic spontaneity.

Other northern wares, Jun and Cizhou, have been produced almost continuously from the Ming dynasty, and are not so much fakes as a continuation of a tradition.

Marks
Factory marks are not found on Chinese stoneware or pottery. However, individual pieces that have been given to a patron or to a temple are found with presentation marks.

Yue wares sometimes feature dates and presentation marks.

Celadon wares are not marked, although some pieces that were bought by Islamic and Indian collectors were dated. This applies especially to celadon dishes which were believed to have the power to neutralize poisons and were very highly regarded.

Cizhou wares were occasionally inscribed by the potter for the recipient of the piece, but there no particular marks were used.

Jun wares are sometimes numbered where a piece is made in two parts, such as a *jardinière*. These types of wares were printed on the base with a number between one and nine in Chinese numerals.

KOREA AND JAPAN
Fakes
Traditional celadons and other stonewares have seen an unbroken line of production, and it is sometimes hard to distinguish older from more recent wares. Especially confusing are bowls made for the tea ceremony: these are so individual that it is very difficult to identify the artist or even the age of a particular piece.

Marks
There are no factory marks on Korean and Japanese pottery.

SOUTH EAST ASIA
Fakes
Fakes of very early Ban Chiang wares from Thailand flooded the market in the 1960s and 1970s. This simple, low-fired ware is very deceptive but the practice did not continue for too long because these piece do not fetch high prices at auction.

Marks
Pottery from Cambodia and Thailand is never marked.

Annamese pottery from Vietnam is sometimes dated: a chronology of wares has been derived from a few pieces, including a bottle found in the Topkapi Palace in Turkey.

ISLAMIC POTTERY
Fakes
Because of the nature of early Islamic pottery – pieces are generally low-fired and crude – it is difficult to identify forgeries, especially turquoise-glazed Kashan wares. But as these are relatively low-priced objects, they do not attract as much attention from forgers as coloured wares, especially Iznik.

In the latter part of the 19thC, the vogue for "Oriental" material generated by the Aesthetic Movement, also included Islamic art, and many copies or imitiations were made.

It is not difficult to identify original Islamic pottery: genuine pieces are made from fine fritware, while copies are made from conventional 19thC European tin-glazed pottery, the pieces are neatly potted, and most items are marked.

Almost every country in Europe produced imitations, the closest by Cantagalli in Florence who made the Iznik tankard shown above, and also by Samson in Paris and De Morgan in England. A genuine version of this type of vessel is shown on p.55. Cantagalli and De Morgan worked together on Iznik and Persian-style wares while De Morgan was living in Florence.

* Be careful because some pieces have had their marks removed by unscrupulous dealers who attempt to pass the items off as original Islamic wares. The base above left, has been gouged out disguising the 19thC maker's mark (see above right).
* Look at colours carefully before deciding whether or not to buy.

Marks
All Islamic pottery features individual potters marks or inscriptions (not factory marks). A number of 16thC Turkish wares were inscribed "Abraham of Kutähya", now a name for a particular style.

SPAIN
Fakes
Spanish potters made fakes of 15thC Hispano-moresque lustre wares, but these tend to have a thinner, denser body, and have a more metallic, higher note when tapped.
* Avoid wares with an even lustre, and smooth, rounded,

unworn edges. Genuine pieces feature natural wear which cannot be replicated by abrasion.
* If the wear is artificial, spiralling abrasion marks will be visible.

Marks
Hispano-moresque and early Spanish wares do not feature factory marks, but later factories do mark pieces along with individual painters.

Alcora (Valencia)
Factory producing tin-glazed wares founded c.1726 by Don Bonaventura Pedro de Alcánara, Count of Aranda with help from workmen from Moustiers. Made creamwares from c.1775. Marks used 1784 or later. Included incised mark:

other "A" marks found appear in brown, black or gold.

PORTUGAL
Fakes
Portuguese pottery has not been widely faked. From the mid-19thC a pottery at Caldas da Rainha made imitations of 16thC Palissy ware.

Marks
Pottery marks were first used in Portugal in the 18thC, when faience was made at a number of centres including Aveiro and Rato near Lisbon.

Aveiro
Faience c.1785:

Caldas da Rainha
Imitation Palissy ware from 1853:

Rato (nr. Lisbon)
Faience 1767-19thC:

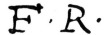

GLOSSARY

Agate ware A type of pottery made by Staffordshire potters in the middle of the 18thC, which is intended to resemble agate by the partial blending of different-coloured clays.

Alafia An Arabic word for "benediction" or "blessing", used symbolically by Moorish potters in early Hispano-moresque lustreware.

Albarello A drug jar, generally of waisted cylindrical form originating in Persia in the 12thC but adopted by almost every major European country from the 15thC on. A variation is the so-called "dumb-bell" form popular in northern Italy, especially in the Veneto.

Alla porcellana Literally "in the style of Chinese blue and white porcelain". A type of scrolling foliage derived from Ming porcelain employed by Italian maiolica decorators in the late 15th and 16thC.

Baluster In ceramics, a term employed to describe a shape of a vase or other vessel, with the profile of an elongated pear or teardrop.

Baroque A European style of Italian origin extending from about 1620 for a little over 100 years. It is a bold decorative style, richly ornamented, sometimes weighty and organic in form or grandly architectural and powerful.

Basaltes Black basaltes, a fine black stoneware developed by Josiah Wedgwood in the 1760s.

Bellarmine A Rhenish stoneware vessel of generally bulbous form with a narrow neck on which is stamped the bearded face associated later with Cardinal Roberto Bellarmino, a stern anti-Protestant. These vessels were made over a long period from the 15th to the beginning of the 19thC. They are termed *bartmannkrug* in Germany.

Berettino A style of decoration initially associated with Faenza from the 1520s on but was later adopted by north Italian potteries, particularly Venice. The object is entirely covered in pale or dark blue tin-glaze which is then painted in white and other colours.

Bianco-di-Faenza A type of maiolica developed in the middle of the 16thC at Faenza. Covered in a thick milk-white glaze, it is usually cursorily decorated in a restricted palette of ochre and blue termed *compendiario*.

Bianco-sopra-bianco Literally "white-on-white". A type of maiolica and later other tin-glazed wares (e.g. Bristol) painted in white enamel on an off-white or bluish ground. The effect is rather like lace-work.

Biscuit Unglazed pottery or porcelain that has been fired only once.

Bisque Another term for biscuit.

Bleu-persan A French adaptation of *berettino* decoration, popular in the latter 17thC at Nevers and copied at Rouen and in England.

Cache-pot A decorative vessel used to enclose a flower-pot.

Cameo A design in contrasting low relief, as found in jasper ware.

Caneware A pale straw-coloured stoneware developed in Staffordshire in the late 18thC and used by many factories including Davenport, Spode and Wedgwood.

Cartouche A decorative panel.

Caudle cup In England the term generally refers to a bulbous side cup used for caudle, a type of spicy, usually milk-based, porridge.

Celadon Green-glaze stoneware so named after a character in a French play who wore a pale green ribbon. Originally made in China during the Song dynasty (960-1279) both in the north and the south of the country it remained popular well into the Ming dynasty. It was also produced in Korea, in Thailand and later in Japan.

Clobbered ware Chinese blue and white porcelain later painted over in Europe in coloured enamels often with the new decoration conflicting with the original theme.

Compendiario The term implies a type of shorthand or abbreviated decoration, it is applied to Faenza maiolica painted in a restricted palette of blue and yellow-ochre, generally with a sketchy design. Popular from about the middle of the 16thC and copied elsewhere.

Coperta A clear lead-glaze superimposed on decorated maiolica to add lustre to the finished product.

Crabstock The form taken by a handle or spout on 18thC English pottery. It is based on the knotty contours of a pruned crab-apple tree.

Creamware Finely potted lead-glazed earthenware developed over along period in the 18thC but brought to refinement by Wedgwood in the 1760s. The paste is a pale straw or cream colour, hence the name.

Delft The name of the town most closely associated with northern tin-glazed earthenware or delft-ware. Although the technique was introduced to the Netherlands by Italian potters probably towards the end of the 15thC, Delft only became prominent from about 1650 onwards.

Enghalskrug Literally a "narrow-necked jug" a type of jug with a bulbous egg-shaped (ovoid) body surmounted by a tall narrow neck. It was popular from about the middle of the 17th for almost a century in Germany and Holland.

Fasackerley A palette associated with Liverpool delftware from about 1750, and which includes a soft sage-green, manganese-brown, pale blue, yellow and red.

Faience Tin-glazed earthenware usually applied to France and Germany and also to later Italian ware. The name is derived from Faenza, one of the biggest pottery making centres in Italy. (Similar to maiolica and delftware).

Feronnerie A type of delicate Baroque scrollwork inspired by wrought-iron work and used on French faience.

Flatbacks Mainly Staffordshire pottery figures and groups made from about 1840 until early in the 20thC. As the name implies the backs are almost flat and undecorated as they were principally intended for the mantelpiece.

Fritware A silicaceous clay bodied ware developed in Persia in the 12thC and used extensively throughout the Islamic world from then on.

Grotesque A fantastical type of ornament originally based on the wall decoration of the underground ruins (*grotte*) of Nero's Golden House rediscovered in about 1480. Raphael and his assistants incorporated these themes into the decorations of the Vatican *Loggie* in 1518/19. They include a wide variety of strange half-human beasts, masks, scrollwork and threads arranged in any number of ways. Other later designers such as Cornelis Bos, Du Cerceau and Jean Berain adapted these motifs in their respective styles.

Ground A monochrome area of surface colour, to which decoration can be added.

Hispano-moresque ware A highly important and influential lustred pottery made in Spain from the 13thC. The main centres were at Malaga in Andalusia and Manises, near Valencia.

Istoriato A school of maiolica painting which arose at the beginning of the 16thC in which the artist uses the dish or vessel as a canvas on which to represent some narrative subject derived from biblical, allegorical, mythological or genre sources, usually via an engraving. The most important centres were Urbino, Castel Durante and Faenza.

Jasper ware A highly-refined white-bodied stoneware used by Josiah Wedgwood from about 1775. Jasper can be stained blue, green, yellow or claret.

Kwaart A thin clear lead-glaze applied over already decorated Dutch delftware to intensify the colours and create a shinier finish. It is equivalent to *coperta* in Italy.

Lambrequin French ornament of the late Baroque period resembling delicate lacework or tracery from borders. This type of decoration was very popular with Rouen potters (and at St. Cloud) at the end of the 17thC and beginning of the 18thC. It is mainly done in cobalt blue, but sometimes is heightened with red.

Lead glaze A clear glaze generally composed of silicaceous sand, salt, soda, potash mixed with a lead component such as litharge (lead monoxide).

Lustre A type of decoration using metallic oxides to produce lustrous surface effects. For example, silver gives a soft golden yellow while copper appears a ruby red colour. These oxides were applied to a fired glazed piece and re-fired at a lower temperature in a reduction kiln. A successful firing would leave a deposit of virtually pure metal on the surface creating the desired lustre. The technique was probably borrowed by Mesopotamian potters from Egyptian glassmakers in the 9thC AD. From then on it was used on Persian, Syrian and Egyptian pottery as well as in post-medieval Spain and Renaissance Italy. The technique was revived by European potters in the latter half of the 19thC.

Luting Joining two or more elements in a ceramic object using a liquid clay or slip "glue".

Maiolica Tin-glazed earthenware produced in Italy from 15th–18thC although tin-glazed ware was made on the peninsula from the 11th or 12thC it was not truly developed until the Renaissance.

Majolica The change of one letter in a corruption of the previous maiolica may appear slight but the material is completely different. Developed by Thomas Minton in the middle of the 19thC it is usually a heavily-potted, complex, moulded type of ware covered in rich but generally sombre coloured lead glazes, including spinach green, dark cobalt blue, brown, ochre often surpisingly in combination

with opaque pastel colours such as turquoise and pink. A number of other factories in England, France, Sweden and north America also made majolica.

Mannerist style A complex and articulate manifestation of the late Renaissance. Employing twisted, exaggerated and bizarre forms often entrapped by strapwork and grotesques, it was highly influential in the decorative arts for almost a century beginning in the 1520s.

Neo-classicism A rational decorative style, almost the antithesis of the rococo style which immediately preceded it. From about 1750 European fine and decorative sought inspiration from classical Greek, Roman or Etruscan architecture and artifacts. In ceramics, forms are clean and simple with unhindered geometric profiles, sometimes embellished in low relief with antique style figures or painted in sombre monochromes with slight architectural type ornamentation. After c.1800 there is a clear move to a heavier type of decoration termed the Empire style which sometimes includes Egyptian elements, a fashion arising from Napoleon's campaigns in north Africa in the 1790s.

Pearl ware A fine earthenware, similar to creamware but with a decided blue tint to the glaze. Although developed by Wedgwood in about 1779 it was soon adopted by all the major potters in England and Wales.

Petit-feu Low-fired enamel colours developed in Germany towards the end of the 17thC and in France in the late 1740s. The palette is much broader than the earlier *grand-feu* colours.

Polychrome Decoration in more than two colours.

Prattware Essentially a creamware decorated in high-fired colours including ochre, yellow, green, brown and blue. Made widely throughout England, Scotland and Wales in the early 19thC.

Press-moulding A modelling technique whereby a figure or object is formed by pressing lumps of clay into moulds.

Raku ware An individually modelled type of earthenware made in Japan for the Tea Ceremony from the late 16thC up to the present day.

Rockingham ware Pottery with a brown glaze, often mottled with yellow, made at Bennington, Vermont in the United States and elsewhere.

Rococo style Sandwiched between the weighty Baroque and the severity of neo-classicism, the rococo style is, at least in terms of the applied arts, an anti-rational style of serpentine planes, delicate conflicting scrolls, with an asymmetrical disposition. It emerged in France towards the end of the 17thC and was superseded by neo-classicism shortly after the middle of the 18thC, although in some countries carried on to the turn of the century.

Ru ware A Chinese Imperial stoneware made towards the end of the northern Song dynasty (960-1127). Thinly potted of pale buff material there is no surface decoration other than a fine duck-egg blue or greenish crackled glaze.

Salt glaze A thinly applied glaze used for covering stonewares. The surface is faintly dimpled, similar to orange skin.

Schnabelkanne (or Schnabelkrug) A Rhenish stoneware jug with a tall diagonally projecting spout resembling a bird's beak. Made at the Siegburg or Raeren potteries in the late 16th and early 17thC.

Schnelle A tall tankard with tapered sides made in the Rhineland, especially at Siegburg, from the 1550s up to about 1600.

Schwarzlot Black enamel painting on faience, porcelain and glass from the latter half of the 17thC on.

Sgraffiato or Sgraffito Literally "scratched" decoration. Usually the design is achieved by cutting through slip or a glaze onto the underlying clay. It is seen on Chinese Cizhou wares, Bolognese pottery, and on English salt-glazed stoneware, among others.

Shufu ware A southern Chinese porcelain with an opaque bluish or greenish glaze made during the Yuan dynasty, apparently partly for official use.

Slip A creamy mixture of clay and water, used to decorate pottery and for slip casting and sprigged wares.

Slip casting The manufacture of thin-bodied vessels using slip in a mould which absorbs the water.

Sprigged ware Pottery decorated with applied slip motifs, mainly vegetation, but occasionally figures during the 18thC.

Spur marks The marks left after the removal of the small stilts used to support pottery during the firing. Dishes usually feature three spur marks.

Stoneware A high-fired pottery composed of clay and ground rock. The latter element vitrifying at temperatures up to 1400°C. First developed in China, probably during the Han dynasty, it was also developed separately in the Rhineland (now Germany) in late medieval Europe.

Terracotta Lightly-fired red earthenware, usually unglazed.

Toby jug A tankard in the form of a seated toper holding a mug of ale. It first appeared in Staffordshire in about 1760. The hat is detachable and forms the lid.

Transfer printing A type of printed decoration, whereby the design of an inked engraving is transferred to paper and from there to the ceramic object.

Trek The Dutch word for the fine outlining, mainly on blue and white wares, mostly done in dark manganese. It is especially noticeable on wares painted in the so-called Chinese "Transitional" style in the latter half of the 17thC.

Wall pocket An 18thC pottery flat-backed vase with small holes for suspension against a wall for the purpose of holding flowers.

Yue ware A southern Chinese green-glazed stoneware made probably from the Han dynasty, or slightly before, to the 10thC.

BIBLIOGRAPHY

Atterbury, Paul J., *European Pottery & Porcelain*, New York 1979

Birks, Tony, *Lucie Rie*, London, 1987

Bly, John (Ed.), *Is It Genuine?: How To Collect Antiques With Confidence*, London, 1986

Caiger-Smith, A., *Tin-Glaze Pottery in Europe and the Islamic World*, London 1973

Charleston, Robert J. (Ed.), *World Ceramics: An Illustrated History*, London 1990

Cushion, J.P. and Honey W.B., *Handbook of Pottery & Porcelain Marks*, London, 1980

Feild, Rachael, *Macdonald Guide To Buying Antique Pottery & Porcelain*, London, 1987; *Victoriana: A Buyer's Guide to the Decorative Arts 1837-1901*, London, 1988

Godden, Geoffrey A., *Encyclopedia of British Pottery and Porcelain Marks*, London, 1964, 1991

Haslam, Malcolm, *Arts & Crafts: A Buyer's Guide to the Decorative Arts in Britain & America 1860-1930*, London, 1988; *Art Nouveau: A Buyer's Guide to the Decorative Arts of the 1900s*, London, 1988; *Art Deco: A Buyer's Guide to the Decorative Arts 1919-1939*, London, 1987

Hecht, Eugene, *After the Fire George Ohr: An American Genius*, Lambertville, New Jersey, 1994

Knowles, Eric, *Victoriana to Art Deco*, London, 1992

Jenyns, S., *Japanese Pottery*, London, 1971

Lane A., *Early Islamic Pottery*, London, 1947; *Later Islamic Pottery*, London, 1957

Lang, Gordon, *European Ceramics at Burghley House*, London, 1991

Lloyd Thomas, E., *Victorian Art Pottery*, London, 1974

The Metropolitan Museum of Art, *19th-Century America, Furniture and Other Decorative Arts*, New York

Miller's Antiques and Collectables: The Facts At Your Fingertips, London, 1993

Miller's Antiques Checklist: Art Deco, London, 1991

Miller's Antiques Checklist: Art Nouveau, London, 1992

Miller's Antiques Checklist: Victoriana, London, 1991

Miller, Judith and Martin, *Understanding Antiques*, London, 1989

Morley, Hugo and McIlroy, Roger, *Christie's Pictorial History of European Pottery*, Oxford, 1984

Piper, Sir David (Ed.), *Dictionary of Art & Artists*, Glasgow, 1988

Rice, Paul and Gowing, Christopher, *British Studio Ceramics in the 20th Century*, London, 1989

Savage, George, Newman, George and Cushion, John, *An Illustrated Dictionary of Ceramics*, London, 1985

Vainker, S.J., *Chinese Pottery & Porcelain*, London, 1991

Watson, Howard, *Collecting Clarice Cliff*, 1988

Wills, Geoffrey, *Wedgwood*, London, 1989

Wilson, T., *Ceramic Art of the Italian Renaissance*, London, 1987

INDEX

ACKNOWLEDGMENTS

The publishers would like to thank the following auction houses, museums, dealers, collectors and other sources for supplying pictures for use in the book.

1 SL; **3** LIO; **16** SL; **20** SL; **21** tlSL, crSL, blSNY; **22** SL; **23** all SL; **24** SL; **25** all SL; **26** SL; **27** all SL; **28** SL; **29** all SL; **30** SL; **31** all SL; **32** SL; **33** all SL; **34** SL; **36** SL; **37** all SL; **38** SL; **39** all SL; **40** SL; **41** tlSNY, trSNY, brSL; **42** SL; **43** all SL; **44** SL; **48** SL; **49** all SL; **50** SL; **51** SL; **52** SL; **53** all SL; **54** SL; **55** all SL; **56** SL; **57** all SL; **58** SL; **60** CNY; **61** tlSL, crCNY, blCNY; **62** SL/IB; **63** all SL; **64** all SL; **65** all SL; **66** SL; **70** SL; **71** all SL; **72** SL/IB; **73** tlSL, crSL, blIB/SL, brSL; **74** SL; **75** all SL; **76** SL; **77** all SL; **78** SL; **90**;all SL; **91** SL; **92** SL; **96** SL; **97** tlSL, trSL, crSL; **98** SL; **99** trSL, clSL, brSL/IB; **100** all SL; **101** all SL; **102** SL; **103** all SL; **104** SL; **105** all SL; **106** SL; **107** clSL/IB, crSL, blSL; **108** GL; **109** tr SL/IB, bSL; **110** all SL; **111** all SL; **112** SL; **118** SL; **119** all SL; **120** all SL; **121** all SL; **122** SL; **123** all SL; **124** SL; **125** all SL; **126** all SL; **127** all SL; **128** SL; **129** tlSL/IB, trSL/IB, blSL, brSL; **130** SL/IB; **131** tlSL/IB, trSL, clSL, brSL; **132** SL; **133** all SL; **134** SL; **135** all SL/IB; **136** SL; **137** all SL; **138** SL; **139** all SL; **140** SL; **141** all SL; **142** SL; **143** tlSL/IB, trLIO, blCSK; **144** CL; **145** all SL; **146** B; **147** all B; **148** B; **149** all B; **150** B; **151** all B; **152** E; **154** E; **155** tlE, crNMD; **156** E; **157** tlE, trNMD, blE; **158** SNY; **159** trSNY, clMMA, brCNY; **160** DR; **161** all DR; **162** all SL; **163** all SL; **166** all SL/IB; **168** SL/IB; **172** SL; **177** SL

KEY
b bottom, c centre, l left, r right

B	Bonhams		Leamington Spa
CL	Christie's London	MMA	Metropolitan
CNY	Christie's New York		Museum of Art,
CSK	Christie's South		New York
	Kensington	NMD	Nicholas M. Dawes
DR	David Rago, Dealer	SL	Sotheby's London
	Auctioneer and	SL/IB	Photography by Ian
	Publisher, Lambertville,		Booth at Sotheby's
	New Jersey		London for Octopus
E	Esto		Publishing Group
GL	Gordon Lang		Ltd.
LIO	Lion's Den,	SNY	Sotheby's New York

The author would like to thank Peter Arney, Colin Mackay, Henry Howard-Sneyd, Simon Cottle, Eric Knowles, Louise Newman and the staff of Sotheby's Educational Studies for their help in preparing this book.

CHECKLIST INFORMATION

MILLER'S ANTIQUES CHECKLISTS are designed to offer collectors a fast and accurate way to identify and date antiques within a particular collecting area. Each one is written by an expert, and details of the authors are given below. On the final page of this book are details of the checklists and a selection of other Miller's titles, together with an order form.

VICTORIANA, ART DECO AND ART NOUVEAU

Eric Knowles is a director of Bonhams, the major London auction house. A leading authority on 19th and 20thC decorative arts, he appears regularly on many television and radio programmes, including the *Antiques Roadshow*, *The Great Antiques Hunt*, *Crimewatch UK* and BBC Radio 2's *Jimmy Young Show*. He has also contributed to a number of other Miller's publications, such as *Miller's Understanding Antiques* and *Victoriana to Art Deco*.

FURNITURE

Richard Davidson is a BADA (British Antiques Dealers Association) furniture dealer in Arundel, West Sussex. He also has a furniture restoration firm, and with his wife and partner, runs a business specializing in the manufacture of fine furniture for the private and professional decorator. He has contributed to a number of publications about antique furniture, including *Miller's Understanding Antiques*.

GLASS

Mark West is a BADA (British Antiques Dealers Association) glass dealer based in Wimbledon in London. He has concentrated on glass collecting for more than 20 years and his shop carries an enormous range, particularly of 18th and 19th century English and continental glassware. He has contributed articles to various specialist publications.

SILVER & PLATE

John Wilson is an acclaimed silver expert and Freeman of the Goldsmith's Company, and has worked in the Silver Department at Sotheby's. His previous work for Miller's includes the section on silver in the best-selling *Miller's Understanding Antiques*.

DOLLS & TEDDY BEARS

Sue Pearson has been a dealer and collector of antique dolls and teddy bears for many years. She has a shop in Brighton and runs a popular doll and teddy bear hospital. She is also a regular contributor to several leading teddy bear magazines.

CLOCKS

John Mighell is the owner of *Strike One*, which has specialized in the restoration and sale of antique clocks and barometers for the past 25 years. He has an extensive knowledge of English, Continental and American clocks, and is the author of numerous articles on clock collecting. He has played a leading role in bringing previously neglected areas of horology, such as tavern clocks and Vienna regulators, to the attention of collectors throughout the world.

TOYS & GAMES

Hugo Marsh is an associate director at Christie's South Kensington, in charge of the Toy Department. He has appeared on the BBC's *Antiques Roadshow* and regularly contributes to antique and collecting magazines. He lives in Oxfordshire.

Other contributors:
Olivia Bristol is an associate director at Christie's South Kensington and is in charge of the Doll Department.
Nigel Mynheer is a consultant at Christie's toy department, and has written several books on toys.
Norman Joplin is one of the country's leading authorities on toy soldiers and is the author of several books on the subject.

SERIES CONSULTANTS

Judith and Martin Miller are internationally famous figures in the world of antiques. In 1979 they set up their own company to produce the annual *Miller's Antiques Price Guide*, which has become the bible of the antiques trade. The guide now has annual sales of over 135,000 copies worldwide.

In the wake of the success of *Miller's Antiques Price Guide*, further best-selling price guides have been produced by Miller's, on pictures, collectables, cars and motorcycles.